C-140

ISBN 0-8373-0140-8

*THE PASSBOOK® SERIES*

# PASSBOOKS®

## FOR

## CAREER OPPORTUNITIES

CLAIMS EXAMINER

# National Learning Corporation

212 Michael Drive, Syosset, New York  11791

(516) 921-8888

Copyright © 1995 by

# National Learning Corporation

212 Michael Drive, Syosset, New York 11791
(516) 921-8888

PRINTED IN THE UNITED STATES OF AMERICA

# PASSBOOK®

## NOTICE

This book is *SOLELY* intended for, is sold *ONLY* to, and its use is *RESTRICTED* to *individual,* bona fide applicants or candidates who qualify by virtue of having seriously filed applications for appropriate license, certificate, professional and/or promotional advancement, higher school matriculation, scholarship, or other legitimate requirements of educational and/or governmental authorities.

This book is *NOT* intended for use, class instruction, tutoring, training, duplication, copying, reprinting, excerption, or adaptation, etc., by:

(1) Other Publishers

(2) Proprietors and/or Instructors of "Coaching" and/or Preparatory Courses

(3) Personnel and/or Training Divisions of commercial, industrial, and governmental organizations

(4) Schools, colleges, or universities and/or their departments and staffs, including teachers and other personnel

(5) Testing Agencies or Bureaus

(6) Study groups which seek by the purchase of a single volume to copy and/or duplicate and/or adapt this material for use by the group as a whole without having purchased individual volumes for each of the members of the group

(7) Et al.

Such persons would be in violation of appropriate Federal and State statutes.

*PROVISION OF LICENSING AGREEMENTS.* — Recognized educational commercial, industrial, and governmental institutions and organizations, and others legitimately engaged in educational pursuits, including training, testing, and measurement activities, may address a request for a licensing agreement to the copyright owners, who will determine whether, and under what conditions, including fees and charges, the materials in this book may be used by them. In other words, a licensing facility *exists* for the legitimate use of the material in this book on other than an individual basis. However, it is asseverated and affirmed here that the materials in this book *CANNOT* be used without the receipt of the express permission of such a licensing agreement from the Publishers.

NATIONAL LEARNING CORPORATION
212 Michael Drive
Syosset, New York 11791

Inquiries re licensing agreements should be addressed to:
The President
National Learning Corporation
212 Michael Drive
Syosset, New York 11791

# PASSBOOK SERIES®

THE *PASSBOOK SERIES®* has been created to prepare applicants and candidates for the ultimate academic battlefield—the examination room.

At some time in our lives, each and every one of us may be required to take an examination—for validation, matriculation, admission, qualification, registration, certification, or licensure.

Based on the assumption that every applicant or candidate has met the basic formal educational standards, has taken the required number of courses, and read the necessary texts, the *PASSBOOK SERIES®* furnishes the one special preparation which may assure passing with confidence, instead of failing with insecurity. Examination questions—together with answers—are furnished as the basic vehicle for study so that the mysteries of the examination and its compounding difficulties may be eliminated or diminished by a sure method.

This book is meant to help you pass your examination provided that you qualify and are serious in your objective.

The entire field is reviewed through the huge store of content information which is succinctly presented through a provocative and challenging approach—the question-and-answer method.

A climate of success is established by furnishing the correct answers at the end of each test.

You soon learn to recognize types of questions, forms of questions, and patterns of questioning. You may even begin to anticipate expected outcomes.

You perceive that many questions are repeated or adapted so that you gain acute insights, which may enable you to score many sure points.

You learn how to confront new questions, or types of questions, and to attack them confidently and work out the correct answers.

You note objectives and emphases, and recognize pitfalls and dangers, so that you may make positive educational adjustments.

Moreover, you are kept fully informed in relation to new concepts, methods, practices, and directions in the field.

You discover that you are actually taking the examination all the time: you are preparing for the examination by "taking" an examination, not by reading extraneous and/or supererogatory textbooks.

In short, this PASSBOOK®, used directedly, should be an important factor in helping you to pass your test.

# CLAIMS EXAMINER

## DUTIES
Investigates, processes, and examiners claims related to torts, workers' compensation, property damages, negligence, and liability cases; performs related duties as required.

## SUBJECT OF EXAMINATION
Written test designed to test for knowledge, skills, and/or abilities in such areas as:
1. Evaluating information and evidence;
2. Using good judgment in conducting investigations;
3. Understanding and interpreting written material; and
4. Preparing written material.

———

# HOW TO TAKE A TEST

I. YOU MUST PASS AN EXAMINATION
   A. *WHAT EVERY CANDIDATE SHOULD KNOW*

   Examination applicants often ask us for help in preparing for the written test.  What can I study in advance?
What kinds of questions will be asked? How will the test be given?
How will the papers be graded?

   As an applicant for a civil service examination, you may be wondering about some of these things. Our purpose here is to suggest effective methods of advance study and to describe civil service examinations.

   Your chances for success on this examination can be increased if you know how to prepare. Those "pre-examination jitters" can be reduced if you know what to expect. You can even experience an adventure in good citizenship if you know why civil service examinations are given.

   B. *WHY ARE CIVIL SERVICE EXAMINATIONS GIVEN?*

   Civil service examinations are important to you in two ways. As a citizen, you want public jobs filled by employees who know how to do their work. As a job-seeker, you want a fair chance to compete for that job on an equal footing with other candidates. The best known means of accomplishing this two-fold goal is the competitive examination.

   Examinations are widely publicized throughout the nation. They may be administered for jobs in federal, state, city, municipal, town, or village governments or agencies.

   Any citizen may apply, with some limitations, such as the age or residence of applicants. Your experience and education may be reviewed to see whether you meet the requirements for the particular examination. When these requirements exist, they are reasonable and are applied consistently to all applicants. Thus, a competitive examination may cause you some uneasiness now, but it is your privilege and safeguard.

   C. *HOW ARE CIVIL SERVICE EXAMINATIONS DEVELOPED?*

   Examinations are carefully written by trained technicians who are specialists in the field known as "psychological measurement," in consultation with recognized authorities in the field of work that the test will cover. These experts recommend the subject matter areas or skills to be tested; only those knowledges or skills important to your success on the job are included. The most reliable books and source materials available are used as references. Together, the experts and technicians judge the difficulty level of the questions.

   Test technicians know how to phrase questions so that the problem is clearly stated. Their ethics do not permit "trick" or "catch" questions. Questions may have been tried out on sample groups, or subjected to statistical analysis, to determine their usefulness.

   Written tests are often used in combination with performance tests, ratings of training and experience, and oral interviews. All of these measures combine to form the best known means of finding the right man for the right job.

## II. HOW TO PASS THE WRITTEN TEST

### A. NATURE OF THE EXAMINATION

To prepare intelligently for civil service examinations, you should know how they differ from school examinations you have taken. In school you were assigned certain definite pages to read or subjects to cover. The examination questions were quite detailed and usually emphasized memory. Civil service examinations, on the other hand, try to discover your present ability to perform the duties of a position, plus your potentiality to learn these duties. In other words, a civil service examination attempts to predict how successful you will be. Questions cover such a broad area that they cannot be as minute and detailed as school examination questions.

In the public service similar kinds of work, or positions, are grouped together in one "class." This process is known as "position-classification." All the positions in a class are paid according to the salary range for that class. One class title covers all these positions, and they are all tested by the same examination.

### B. FOUR BASIC STEPS

1. Study the Announcement.--How, then, can you know what subjects to study? Our best answer is: "Learn as much as possible about the class of positions for which you have applied." The examination will test the knowledge, skills, and abilities needed to do the work.

Your most valuable source of information about the position you want is the official announcement of the examination. This announcement lists the training and experience qualifications. Check these standards and apply only if you come reasonably close to meeting them.

The brief description of the position in the examination announcement offers some clues to the subjects which will be tested. Think about the job itself. Review the duties in your mind. Can you perform them, or are there some in which you are rusty?  Fill in the blank spots in your preparation.

Many jurisdictions preview the written test in the examination announcement by including a section called "Knowledge and Abilities Required," "Scope of Examination," or some similar heading. Here you will find out specifically what fields will be tested.

2. Review Your Own Background.-- Once you learn in general what the position is all about, and what you need to know to do the work, ask yourself which subjects you already know fairly well and which need improvement. You may wonder whether to concentrate on improving your strong areas or on building some background in your fields of weakness. When the announcement has specified "some knowledge" or "considerable knowledge," or has used adjectives such as "beginning principles of ...." or "advanced .....methods," you can get a clue as to the number and difficulty of questions to be asked in any given field. More questions, and hence broader coverage, would be included for those subjects which are more important in the work. Now weigh your strengths and weaknesses against the job requirements and prepare accordingly.

3. Determine the Level of the Position.-- Another way to tell how intensively you should prepare is to understand the level of the job for which you are applying. Is it the entering level? In other words, is this the position in which beginners in a field of work are hired? Or is it an intermediate or advanced level? Sometimes this is indicated by such words as "Junior" or "Senior" in the class title.Other jurisdictions use Roman numerals to designate the level: Clerk I,

Clerk II, for example. The word "Supervisor" sometimes appears in the title. If the level is not indicated by the title, check the description of duties. Will you be working under very close supervision, or will you have responsibility for independent decisions in this work?

    4. Choose Appropriate Study Materials.-- Now that you know the subjects to be examined and the relative amount of each subject to be covered, you can choose suitable study materials. For beginning level jobs, or even advanced ones, if you have a pronounced weakness in some aspect of your training, read a modern, standard textbook in that field. Be sure it is up-to-date and has general coverage. Such books are normally available at your library, and the librarian will be glad to help you locate one. For entry level positions, questions of appropriate difficulty are chosen -- neither highly advanced questions, nor those too simple. Such questions require careful thought but not advanced training.

    If the position for which you are applying is technical or advanced, you will read more advanced, specialized material. If you are already familiar with the basic principles of your field, elementary textbooks would waste your time. Concentrate on advanced textbooks and technical periodicals. Think through the concepts and review difficult problems in your field.

    These are all general sources. You can get more ideas on your own initiative, following these leads. For example, training manuals and publications of the government agency which employs workers in your field can be useful, particularly for technical and professional positions. A letter or visit to the government department involved may result in more specific study suggestions, and certainly will provide you with a more definite idea of the exact nature of the position you are seeking.

II. KINDS OF TESTS

    Tests are used for purposes other than measuring knowledge and ability to perform specified duties. For some positions, it is equally important to test ability to make adjustments to new situations or to profit from training. In others, basic mental abilities not dependent upon information are essential. Questions which test these things may not appear as pertinent to the duties of the position as those which test for knowledge and information. Yet they are often highly important parts of a fair examination. For very general questions, it is almost impossible to help you direct your study efforts. What we can do is to point out some of the more common of these general abilities needed in public service positions and describe some typical questions.

    1. General Information

        Broad, general information has been found useful for predicting job success in some kinds of work. This is tested in a variety of ways, from vocabulary lists to questions about current events. Basic background in some field of work, such as sociology or economics, may be sampled in a group of questions. Often these are principles which have become familiar to most persons through "exposure" rather than through formal training. It is difficult to advise you how to study for these questions; being alert to the world around you is our best suggestion.

2. Verbal Ability

An example of an ability needed in many positions is verbal or language ability. Verbal ability is, in brief, the ability to use and understand words. Vocabulary and grammar tests are typical measures of this ability. "Reading comprehension" or "paragraph interpretation" questions are common in many kinds of civil service tests. You are given a paragraph of written material and asked to find its central meaning.

3. Numerical Ability

Number skills can be tested by the familiar arithmetic problem, by checking paired lists of numbers to see which are alike and which are different, or by interpreting charts and graphs. In the latter test, a graph may be printed in the test booklet which you are asked to use as the basis for answering questions.

4. Observation

A popular test for law-enforcement positions is the observation test. A picture is shown to you for several minutes, then taken away. Questions about the picture test your ability to observe both details and larger elements.

5. Following Directions

In many positions in the public service, the employee must be able to carry out written instructions dependably and accurately. You may be given a chart with several columns, each column listing a variety of information. The questions require you to carry out directions involving the information given in the chart.

6. Skills and Aptitudes

Performance tests effectively measure some manual skills and aptitudes. When the skill is one in which you are trained, such as typing or shorthand, you can practice. These tests are often very much like those given in business school or high school courses. For many of the other skills and aptitudes, however, no short-time preparation can be made. Skills and abilities natural to you or that you have developed throughout your lifetime are being tested.

Many of the general questions just described provide all the data needed to answer the questions and ask you to use your reasoning ability to find the answers. Your best preparation for these tests, as well as for tests of facts and ideas, is to be at your physical and mental best.  You, no doubt, have your own methods of getting into an exam-taking mood and keeping "in shape."  The next section lists some ideas on this subject.

IV. KINDS OF QUESTIONS

Only rarely is the "essay" question, which you answer in narrative form, used in civil service tests.  Civil service tests are usually of the short-answer type. Full instructions for answering these questions will be given to you at the examination. But in case this is your first experience with short-answer questions and separate answer sheets, here is what you need to know.

1. Multiple-Choice Questions

Most popular of the short-answer questions is the "multiple-choice" or "best-answer" question. It can be used, for example, to test for factual knowledge, ability to solve problems, or judgment in meeting situations found at work.

A multiple-choice question is normally one of three types:

(1) It can begin with an incomplete statement followed by several possible endings. You are to find the one ending which *best* completes the statement, although some of the others may not be entirely wrong.

(2) It can also be a complete statement in the form of a question which is answered by choosing one of the statements listed.

(3) It can be in the form of a problem -- again you select the best answer.

Here is an example of a multiple-choice question with a discussion which should give you some clues as to the method for choosing the right answer.

SAMPLE QUESTION:

When an employee has a complaint about his assignment, the action which will *best* help him overcome his difficulty is

    (A) to discuss his difficulty with his co-workers
    (B) to take the problem to the head of the organization
    (C) to take the problem to the person who gave him the
        assignment
    (D) to say nothing to anyone about his complaint

In answering this question you should study each of the choices to find which is best. Consider choice (A). Certainly an employee may discuss his complaint with fellow employees, but no change or improvement can result, and the complaint remains unsolved. Choice (B) is a poor choice since the head of the organization probably does not know what assignment you have been given, and taking your problem to him is known as "going over the head" of the supervisor. The supervisor, or person who made the assignment, is the person who can clarify it or correct any injustice. Choice (C) is, therefore, correct. To say nothing, as in choice (D), is unwise. Supervisors have an interest in knowing the problems employees are facing, and the employee is seeking a solution to his problem.

2. True-False Questions

The "true-false" or "right-wrong" form of question is sometimes used. Here a complete statement is given. Your problem is to decide whether the statement is right or wrong.

SAMPLE QUESTION:

A person-to-person long distance telephone call costs less than a station-to-station call to the same city.

This question is wrong, or "false," since person-to-person calls are more expensive.

This is not a complete list of all possible question forms, although most of the others are variations of these common types. You will always get complete directions for answering questions. Be sure you understand *how* to mark your answers -- ask questions until you do.

V. RECORDING YOUR ANSWERS

For an examination with very few applicants, you may be told to record your answers in the test booklet itself. Separate answer sheets are much more common. If this separate answer sheet is to be scored by machine -- and this is often the case -- it is highly important that you mark your answers correctly in order to get credit.

An electric test-scoring machine is often used in civil service offices because of the speed with which papers can be scored. Machine-scored answer sheets must be marked with a special pencil, which will be given to you. This pencil has a high graphite content which responds to the electrical scoring machine. As a matter of fact, stray dots may register as answers, so do not let your pencil rest on the answer sheet while you are pondering the correct answer. Also, if your pencil lead breaks or is otherwise defective, ask for another.

Since the answer sheet will be dropped in a slot in the scoring machine, be careful not to bend the corners or get the paper crumpled.

The answer sheet normally has five vertical columns of numbers, with 30 numbers to a column. These numbers correspond to the question numbers in your test booklet. After each number, going across the page, are four or five pairs of dotted lines. These short dotted lines have small letters or numbers above them. The first two pairs may also have a "T" and "F" above the letters. This indicates that the first two pairs only are to be used if the questions are of the true-false type. If the questions are multiple-choice, disregard this "T" and "F" completely, and pay attention only to the small number or letters.

Answer your questions in the manner of the sample that follows. Proceed in the sequential steps outlined below.

Assume that you are answering question 32, which is:

32. The largest city in the United States is:
    A. Washington, D.C.    B. New York City    C. Chicago
    D. Detroit    E. San Francisco

1. Choose the answer you think is best.
   New York City is the largest, so choice B is correct.
2. Find the row of dotted lines numbered the same as the question you are answering.
   This is question number 32, so find row number 32.
3. Find the pair of dotted lines corresponding to the answer you have chosen.
   You have chosen answer B, so find the pair of dotted lines marked "B".
4. Make a solid black mark between the dotted lines.
   Go up and down two or three times with your pencil so plenty of graphite rubs off, but do not let the mark get outside or above the dots.

## VI. BEFORE THE TEST

Common sense will help you find procedures to follow to get ready for an examination. Too many of us, however, overlook these sensible measures. Indeed, nervousness and fatigue have been found to be the most serious reasons why applicants fail to do their best on civil service tests. Here is a list of reminders.

1. Begin Your Preparation Early

Don't wait until the last minute to go scurrying around for books and materials or to find out what the position is all about.

2. Prepare Continuously

An hour a night for a week is better than an all-night cram session. This has been definitely established. What is more, a night a week for a month will return better dividends than crowding your study into a shorter period of time.

3. Locate the Place of the Examination

You have been sent a notice telling you when and where to report for the examination. If the location is in a different town or otherwise unfamiliar to you, it would be well to inquire the best route and learn something about the building.

4. Relax the Night Before the Test

Allow your mind to rest. Do not study at all that night. Plan some mild recreation or diversion; then go to bed early and get a good night's sleep.

5. Get Up Early Enough to Make a Leisurely Trip to the Place for the Test

Then unforeseen events, traffic snarls, unfamiliar buildings, will not upset you.

6. Dress Comfortably

A written test is not a fashion show. You will be known by number and not by name, so wear something comfortable.

7. Leave Excess Paraphernalia at Home

Shopping bags and odd bundles will get in your way. You need bring only the items mentioned in the official notice sent to you; usually everything you need is provided. Do not bring reference books to the examination. They will only confuse those last minutes and be taken away from you when in the test room.

8. Arrive Somewhat Ahead of Time

If because of transportation schedules you must get there very early, bring a newspaper or magazine to take your mind off yourself while waiting.

9. Locate the Examination Room

When you have found the proper room, you will be directed to the seat or part of the room where you will sit. Sometimes you are given a sheet of instructions to read while you are waiting. Do not fill out any forms until you are told to do so; just read them and be ready.

10. Relax and Prepare to Listen to the Instructions

11. If you have any physical problem that may keep you from doing your best, be sure to tell the test administrator. If you are sick, or in poor health, you really cannot do your best on the test. You can come back and take the test some other time.

VII.  AT THE TEST

The day of the test is here and you have the test booklet in your hand. The temptation to get going is very strong. Caution! There is more to success than knowing the right answers. You must know how to identify your papers and understand variations in the type of short-answer question used in this particular examination. Follow these suggestions for maximum results from your efforts:

1. Cooperate with the Monitor

The test administrator has a duty to create a situation in which you can be as much at ease as possible. He will give instructions, tell you when to begin, check to see that you are marking your answer sheet correctly. He is not there to guard you, although he will see that your competitors do not take unfair advantage. He wants to help you do your best.

2. Listen to All Instructions

Don't jump the gun! Wait until you understand all directions. In most civil service tests you get more time than you need to answer the questions. So don't get in a hurry. Read each word of instructions until you clearly understand the meaning. Study the examples. Listen to all announcements. Follow directions. Ask questions if you do not understand what to do.

3. Identify Your Papers

Civil service examinations are usually identified by number only. You will be assigned a number; you must not put your name on your test papers. Be sure to copy your number correctly. Since more than one examination may be given, copy your exact examination title.

4. Plan Your Time

Unless you are told that a test is a "speed" or "rate-of-work" test, speed itself is not usually important. Time enough to answer all the questions will be provided. But this does not mean that you have all day. An overall time limit has been set. Divide the total time (in minutes) by the number of questions to get the approximate time you have for each question.

5. Do Not Linger Over Difficult Questions

If you come across a difficult question, mark it with a paper clip (useful to have along) and come back to it when you have been through the booklet. One caution if you do this -- be sure to skip a number on your answer sheet too.  Check often to be sure that you have not lost your place and that you are marking in the row numbered the same as the question you are answering.

6. Read the Questions

Be sure you know what the question asks!  Many capable people are unsuccessful because they failed to *read* the questions correctly.

7. Answer All Questions

Unless you have been instructed that a penalty will be deducted for incorrect answers, it is better to guess than to omit a question.

8. Speed Tests

It is often better *not* to guess on speed tests. It has been found that on timed tests people are tempted to spend the last few seconds before time is called in marking answers at random -- without even reading them -- in the hope of picking up a few extra points. To discourage this practice, the instructions may warn you that your score will be "corrected" for guessing. That is, a penalty will be applied. The incorrect answers will be deducted from the correct ones, or some other penalty formula will be used.

9. Review Your Answers

If you finish before time is called, go back to the questions you guessed or omitted to give further thought to them. Review other answers if you have time.

10. Return Your Test Materials

If you are ready to leave before others have finished or time is called, take *all* your materials to the monitor and leave quietly. Never take any test material with you. The monitor can discover whose papers are not complete, and taking a test booklet may be grounds for disqualification.

## VIII. EXAMINATION TECHNIQUES

1. Read the *general* instructions carefully. These are usually printed on the first page of the examination booklet. As a rule, these instructions refer to the timing of the examination; the fact that you should not start work until the signal and must stop work at a signal, etc. If there are any *special* instructions, such as a choice of questions to be answered, make sure that you note this instruction carefully.

2. When you are ready to start work on the examination, that is as soon as the signal has been given, read the instructions to each question booklet, underline any key words or phrases, such as *least, best, outline, describe,* and the like. In this way you will tend to answer as requested rather than discover on reviewing your paper that you *listed without describing,* that you selected the *worst* choice rather than the *best* choice, etc.

3. If the examination is of the objective or so-called multiple-choice type, that is, each question will also give a series of possible answers: A, B, C, or D, and you are called upon to select the best answer and write the letter next to that answer on your answer paper, it is advisable to start answering each question in turn. There may be anywhere from 50 to 100 such questions in the three or four hours allotted and you can see how much time would be taken if you read through all the questions before beginning to answer any. Furthermore, if you come across a question or a group of questions which you know would be difficult to answer, it would undoubtedly affect your handling of all the other questions.

4. If the examination is of the esssay-type and contains but a few questions, it is a moot point as to whether you should read all the questions before starting to answer any one. Of course if you are given a choice, say five out of seven and the like, then it is essential to read all the questions so you can eliminate the two which are most difficult. If, however, you are asked to answer all the questions, there may be danger in trying to answer the easiest one first because you may find that you will spend too much time on it. The best technique is to answer the first question, then proceed to the second, etc.

5. Time your answers. Before the examination begins, write down the time it started, then add the time allowed for the examination and write down the time it must be completed, then divide the time available somewhat as follows:

(a) If $3\frac{1}{2}$ hours are allowed, that would be 210 minutes. If you have 80 objective-type questions, that would be an average of $2\frac{1}{2}$ minutes per question. Allow yourself no more than 2 minutes per question, or a total of 160 minutes, which will permit about 50 minutes to review.

(b) If for the time allotment of 210 minutes, there are 7 essay questions to answer, that would average about 30 minutes a question. Give yourself only 25 minutes per question so that you have about 35 minutes to review.

6. The most important instruction is *to read each question* and make sure you know what is wanted. The second most important instruction is to *time yourself properly* so that you answer every question. The third most important instruction is to *answer every question*. Guess if you have to but include something for each question. Remember that you will receive no credit for a blank and will probably receive some credit if you write something in answer to an essay question. If you guess a letter, say "B" for a multiple-choice question, you may have guessed right. If you leave a blank as the answer to a multiple-choice question, the examiners may respect your feelings but it will not add a point to your score.

7. Suggestions
   a. Objective-Type Questions
      (1) Examine the question booklet for proper sequence of pages and questions.
      (2) Read all instructions carefully.
      (3) Skip any question which seems too difficult; return to it after all other questions have been answered.
      (4) Apportion your time properly; do not spend too much time on any single question or group of questions.
      (5) Note and underline key words -- *all, most, fewest, least, best, worst, same, opposite*.
      (6) Pay particular attention to negatives.
      (7) Note unusual option, e.g., unduly long, short, complex, different or similar in content to the body of the question.
      (8) Observe the use of "hedging" words -- *probably, may, most likely, etc.*
      (9) Make sure that your answer is put next to the same number as the question.
      (10) Do not second-guess unless you have good reason to believe the second answer is definitely more correct.
      (11) Cross out original answer if you decide another answer is more accurate; do not erase.
      (12) Answer all questions; guess unless instructed otherwise.
      (13) Leave time for review.
   b. Essay-Type Questions
      (1) Read each question carefully.
      (2) Determine exactly what is wanted. Underline key words or phrases.
      (3) Decide on outline or paragraph answer.
      (4) Include many different points and elements unless asked to develop any one or two points or elements.
      (5) Show impartiality by giving pros and cons unless directed to select one side only.
      (6) Make and write down any assumptions you find necessary to answer the question.
      (7) Watch your English, grammar, punctuation, choice of words.
      (8) Time your answers; don't crowd material.

8. Answering the Essay Question
   Most essay questions can be answered by framing the specific response around several key words or ideas. Here are a few such key words or ideas:

M's: manpower, materials, methods, money, management;
P's: purpose, program, policy, plan, procedure, practice, problems, pitfalls, personnel, public relations.

a. Six Basic Steps in Handling Problems:
   (1) Preliminary plan and background development
   (2) Collect information, data and facts
   (3) Analyze and interpret information, data and facts
   (4) Analyze and develop solutions as well as make recommendations
   (5) Prepare report and sell recommendations
   (6) Install recommendations and follow up effectiveness

b. Pitfalls to Avoid
   (1) *Taking things for granted*
      A statement of the situation does not necessarily imply that each of the elements is necessarily true; for example, a complaint may be invalid and biased so that all that can be taken for granted is that a complaint has been registered.
   (2) *Considering only one side of a situation*
      Wherever possible, indicate several alternatives and then point out the reasons you selected the best one.
   (3) *Failing to indicate follow-up*
      Whenever your answer indicates action on your part, make certain that you will take proper follow-up action to see how successful your recommendations, procedures, or actions turn out to be.
   (4) *Taking too long in answering any single question*
      Remember to time your answers properly.

IX. AFTER THE TEST

Scoring procedures differ in detail among civil service jurisdictions although the general principles are the same. Whether the papers are hand-scored or graded by the electric scoring machine we have described, they are nearly always graded by number. That is, the person who marks the paper knows only the number -- never the name -- of the applicant. Not until all the papers have been graded will they be matched with names. If other tests, such as training and experience or oral interview ratings have been given, scores will be combined. Different parts of the examination usually have different weights. For example, the written test might count 60 percent of the final grade, and a rating of training and experience 40 percent. In many jurisdictions, veterans will have a certain number of points added to their grades.

After the final grade has been determined, the names are placed in grade order and an eligible list is established. There are various methods for resolving ties between those who get the same final grade: probably the most common is to place first the name of the person whose application was received first. Job offers are made from the eligible list in the order the names appear on it.

You will be notified of your grade and your rank order as soon as all these computations have been made. This will be done as rapidly as possible.

People who are found to meet the requirements in the announcement are called "eligibles." Their names are put on a list of eligibles. An eligible's chances of getting a job depend on how high he stands on this list and how fast agencies are filling jobs from the list.

When a job is to be filled from a list of eligibles, the agency asks for the names of people on the list of eligibles for that job.

When the civil service commission receives this request, it sends to the agency the names of the three people highest on the list. Or, if the job to be filled has specialized requirements, the office sends the agency, from the general list, the names of the top three persons who meet those requirements.

The appointing officer makes a choice from among the three people whose names were sent to him. If the selected person accepts the appointment, the names of the others are put back on the list to be considered for future openings.

That is the rule in hiring from all kinds of eligible lists, whether they are for typist, carpenter, chemist, or something else. For every vacancy, the appointing officer has his choice of any one of the top three eligibles on the list. This explains why the person whose name is on top of the list sometimes does not get an appointment when some of the persons lower on the list do. If the appointing officer chooses the No.2 or No.3 eligible, the No.1 eligible does not get a job at once, but stays on the list until he is appointed or the list is terminated.

X. HOW TO PASS THE INTERVIEW TEST

The examination for which you applied requires an oral interview test. You have already taken the written test and you are now being called for the interview test -- the final part of the formal examination.

You may think that it is not possible to prepare for an interview test and that there are no procedures to follow during an interview.

Our purpose is to point out some things you can do in advance that will help you and some good rules to follow and pitfalls to avoid while you are being interviewed.

A. WHAT IS AN INTERVIEW SUPPOSED TO TEST?

The written examination is designed to test the technical knowledge and competence of the candidate; the oral is designed to evaluate intangible qualities, not readily measured otherwise, and to establish a list showing the relative fitness of each candidate, *as measured against his competitors,* for the position sought. Scoring is not on the basis of "right" or "wrong," but on a sliding scale of values ranging from "not passable" to "outstanding." As a matter of fact, it is possible to achieve a relatively low score without a single "incorrect" answer because of evident weakness in the qualities being measured,

Occasionally, an examination may consist entirely of an oral test -- either an individual or a group oral. In such cases, information is sought concerning the technical knowledges and abilities of the candidate, since there has been no written examination for this purpose. More commonly, however, an oral test is used to supplement a written examination.

B. WHO CONDUCTS INTERVIEWS?

The composition of oral boards varies among different jurisdictions. In nearly all, a representative of the personnel department serves as chairman. One of the members of the board may be a representative of the department in which the candidate would work. In some cases, "outside experts" are used, and frequently a business man or some other representative of the general public is asked to serve. Labor and management or other special groups may be represented. The aim is to secure the services of experts in the appropriate field.

However the board is composed, it is a good idea (and not at all improper or unethical) to ascertain in advance of the interview who the members are and what groups they represent. When you are introduced to them, you will have some idea of their backgrounds and interests, and at least you will not stutter and stammer over their names.

## C. WHAT TO DO BEFORE THE INTERVIEW

While knowledge about the board members is useful and takes some of the surprise element out of the interview, there is other preparation which is more substantive. It *is* possible to prepare for an oral -- in several ways:

1. Keep a Copy of Your Application and Review it Carefully Before the Interview

   This may be the only document before the oral board, and the starting point of the interview. Know what experience and education you have listed there, and the sequence and dates of it. Sometimes the board will ask *you* to review the highlights of your experience for them; you should not have to hem and haw doing it.

2. Study the Class Specification and the Examination Announcement

   Usually, the oral board has one or both of these to guide them. The qualities, characteristics, or knowledges required by the position sought are stated in these documents. They offer valuable clues as to the nature of the oral interview. For example, if the job involves supervisory responsibilities, the announcement will usually indicate that knowledge of modern supervisory methods and the qualifications of the candidate as a supervisor will be tested. If so, you can expect such questions, frequently in the form of a hypothetical situation which you are expected to solve. *Never* go into an oral without knowledge of the duties and responsibilities of the job you seek.

3. Think Through Each Qualification Required

   Try to visualize the kind of questions *you* would ask if you were a board member. How well could you answer them? Try especially to appraise your own knowledge and background in each area, *measured against the job sought,* and identify any areas in which you are weak. Be critical and realistic -- do not flatter yourself.

4. Do Some General Reading in Areas in Which You Feel You May be Weak

   For example, if the job involves supervision and your past experience has *not,* some general reading in supervisory methods and practices, particularly in the field of human relations, might be useful. *Do not* study agency procedures or detailed manuals. The oral board will be testing your understanding and capacity, *not* your memory.

5. Get a Good Night's Sleep and Watch Your General Health and Mental Attitude

   You will want a clear head at the interview. Take care of a cold or other minor ailment, and, of course, *no hangovers.*

*D. WHAT TO DO THE DAY OF THE INTERVIEW*

Now comes the day of the interview itself. Give yourself plenty
of time to get there. Plan to arrive somewhat ahead of the scheduled
time, particularly if your appointment is in the fore part of the
day. If a previous candidate fails to appear, the board might be ready
for you a bit early. By early afternoon an oral board is almost in-
variably behind schedule if there are many candidates, and you may
have to wait. Take along a book or magazine to read, or your application to review. But leave any extraneous material in the waiting
room when you go in for your interview. In any event, relax and com-
pose yourself.

The matter of dress is important. The board is forming impres-
sions about you -- from your experience, your manners, your attitudes, and from your appearance. Give your personal appearance careful attention. Dress your *best*, but not your flashiest. Choose con-
servative, appropriate clothing, and be sure it and you are immacu-
late. This is a business interview, and your appearance should indicate that you regard it as such. Besides, being well-groomed and properly dressed will help boost your confidence.

Sooner or later, someone will call your name and escort you into the interview room. *This is it.* From here on you are on your own.
It is too late for any more preparation. But, remember, you asked for
this opportunity to prove your fitness, and you are here because your
request was granted.

*E. WHAT HAPPENS WHEN YOU GO IN?*

The usual sequence of events will be as follows: The clerk (who
is often the board stenographer) will introduce you to the chairman
of the oral board, who will introduce you to each other member of
the board. Acknowledge the introductions before you sit down. Do not
be surprised if you find a microphone facing you or a stenotypist sit-
ting by. Oral interviews are usually recorded, in the event of an ap-
peal or other review.

Usually the chairman of the board will open the interview by reviewing the highlights of your education and work experience from
your application -- primarily for the benefit of the other members
of the board, as well as to get the material into the record. Do not
interrupt or comment unless there is an error or significant misin-
terpretation; if so, do not hesitate. But do not quibble about in-
significant matters. Usually, also, he will ask you some question
about your education, your experience, or your present job -- partly
to get you started talking, to establish the interviewing "rapport."
He may start the actual questioning, or turn it over to one of the
other members. Frequently each member undertakes the questioning on
a particular area, one in which he is perhaps most competent. So you
can expect each member to participate in the examination. And because the time is limited, you may expect some rather abrupt switches
in the direction the questioning takes. Do not be upset by it. Normally, a board member will not pursue a single line of questioning
unless he discovers a particular strength or weakness.

After each member has participated, the chairman will usually
ask whether any member has any further questions, then will ask you
if you have anything you wish to add. Unless you are expecting this
question, it may floor you. Or worse, it may start you off on an extended, extemporaneous speech. The board is not usually seeking more
information. The question is principally to offer you a last opportunity to present further qualifications or to indicate that you have

nothing to add. So, if you feel that a significant qualification or characteristic has been overlooked, it is proper to point it out in a sentence or so. Do not compliment the board on the thoroughness of their examination -- they have been sketchy, and you know it. If you wish, merely say, "No thank you, I have nothing further to add." This is a point where you can "talk yourself out" of a good impression or fail to present an important bit of information. *Remember, you close the interview yourself.*

The chairman will then say,"That is all,Mr.Smith,thank you." Do not be startled; the interview is over, and quicker than you think. Say,"Thank you and good morning," gather up your belongings and take your leave. Save your sigh of relief for the other side of the door.

F. *HOW TO PUT YOUR BEST FOOT FORWARD*

Throughout all this process, you may feel that the board individually and collectively is trying to pierce your defenses, to seek out your hidden weaknesses, and to embarrass and confuse you. Actually, this is not true. They are obliged to make an appraisal of your qualifications for the job you are seeking, and they *want to see you in your best light*. Remember, they must interview all candidates and a noncooperative candidate may become a failure in spite of their best efforts to bring out his qualifications. Here are fifteen(15) suggestions that will help you:

1. Be Natural.  Keep Your Attitude Confident,But Not Cocky

If *you* are not confident that you can do the job, do not ex-expect the *board* to be. Do not apologize for your weaknesses, try to bring out your strong points. The board is interested in a positive, not a negative presentation. Cockiness will antagonize any board member, and make him wonder if you are covering up a weakness by a false show of strength.

2. Get Comfortable, But Don't Lounge or Sprawl

Sit erectly but not stiffly. A careless posture may lead the board to conclude you are careless in other things, or at least that you are not impressed by the importance of the occasion to you.Either conclusion is natural, even if incorrect. Do not fuss with your clothing, or with a pencil or an ashtray. Your hands may occasionally be useful to emphasize a point; do not let them become a point of distraction.

3. Do Not Wisecrack or Make Small Talk

This is a serious situation, and your attitude should show that you consider it as such. Further, the time of the board is limited; they do not want to waste it, and neither should you.

4. Do Not Exaggerate Your Experience or Abilities

In the first place, from information in the application,from other interviews and other sources, the board may know more about you than you think; in the second place, you probably will not get away with it in the first place. An experienced board is rather adept at spotting such a situation. Do not take the chance.

5. If You Know a Member of the Board, Do Not Make a Point of It, Yet Do Not Hide It.

Certainly you are not fooling him, and probably not the other members of the board. Do not try to take advantage of your acquainceship -- it will probably do you little good.

6. Do Not Dominate the Interview

Let the board do that. They will give you the clues -- do not assume that you have to do all the talking. Realize that the board has a number of questions to ask you, and do not try to take up all the interview time by showing off your extensive knowledge of the answer to the first one.

### 7. Be Attentive

You only have twenty minutes or so, and you should keep your attention at its sharpest throughout. When a member is addressing a problem or a question to you, give him your undivided attention. Address your reply principally to him, but do not exclude the other members of the board.

### 8. Do Not Interrupt

A board member may be stating a problem for you to analyze. He will ask you a question when the time comes. Let him state the problem, and wait for the question.

### 9. Make Sure You Understand the Question

Do not try to answer until you are sure what the question is. If it is not clear, restate it in your own words or ask the board member to clarify it for you. But do not haggle about minor elements.

### 10. Reply Promptly But Not Hastily

A common entry on oral board rating sheets is "candidate responded readily," or "candidate hesitated in replies." Respond as promptly and quickly as you can, but do not jump to a hasty, ill-considered answer.

### 11. Do Not Be Peremptory in Your Answers

A brief answer is proper -- but do not fire your answer back. That is a losing game from your point of view. The board member can probably ask questions much faster than you can answer them.

### 12. Do Not Try To Create the Answer You Think the Board Member Wants

He is interested in what kind of mind you have and how it works -- not in playing games. Furthermore, he can usually spot this practice and will usually grade you down on it.

### 13. Do Not Switch Sides in Your Reply Merely to Agree With a Board Member

Frequently, a member will take a contrary position merely to draw you out and to see if you are willing and able to defend your point of view. Do not start a debate, yet do not surrender a good position. If a position is worth taking, it is worth defending.

### 14. Do Not Be Afraid to Admit an Error in Judgment if You Are Shown to Be Wrong

The board knows that you are forced to reply without any opportunity for careful consideration. Your answer may be demonstrably wrong. If so, admit it and get on with the interview.

### 15. Do Not Dwell at Length on Your Present Job

The opening question may relate to your present assignment. Answer the question but do not go into an extended discussion. You are being examined for a *new* job, not your present one. As a matter of fact, try to phrase *all* your answers in terms of the job for which you are being examined.

## G. BASIS OF RATING

Probably you will forget most of these "do's" and "don'ts" when you walk into the oral interview room. Even remembering them all will not insure you a passing grade. Perhaps you did not have the qualifications in the first place. But remembering them *will* help you to put your best foot forward, without treading on the toes of the board members.

Rumor and popular opinion to the contrary notwithstanding, an oral board wants you to make the best appearance possible. They know you are under pressure -- but they also want to see how you respond to it as a guide to what your reaction would be under the pressures of the job you seek. They will be influenced by the degree of poise you display, the personal traits you show, and the manner in which you respond.

# EXAMINATION SECTION

# EXAMINATION SECTION

DIRECTIONS: Each question or incomplete statement is followed by
several suggested answers or completions. Select the
one that BEST answers the question or completes the
statement. *PRINT THE LETTER OF THE CORRECT ANSWER IN
THE SPACE AT THE RIGHT.*

1. The reliability of information obtained increases with the       1.___
number of persons interviewed. The more the interviewees
differ in their statements, the more persons it is necessary
to interview to ascertain the true facts.
According to this statement, the dependability of the
information about an occurrence obtained from interviews is
related to
   A. how many people are interviewed
   B. how soon after the occurrence an interview can be
   arranged
   C. the individual technique of the interviewer
   D. the interviewer's ability to detect differences in the
   statements of interviewees

2. A sufficient quantity of the material supplied as evidence       2.___
enables the laboratory expert to determine the true nature
of the substance, whereas an extremely limited specimen may
be an abnormal sample containing foreign matter not indica-
tive of the true nature of the material.
On the basis of this statement alone, it may be concluded
that a reason for giving an adequate sample of material for
evidence to a laboratory expert is that
   A. a limited specimen spoils more quickly than a larger
   sample
   B. a small sample may not truly represent the evidence
   C. he cannot analyze a small sample correctly
   D. he must have enough material to keep a part of it
   untouched to show in court

Questions 3-4.

DIRECTIONS: Questions 3 and 4 are based ONLY on the information
given in the following paragraph.

*Credibility of a witness is usually governed by his character
and is evidenced by his reputation for truthfulness. Personal or
financial reasons or a criminal record may cause a witness to give
false information to avoid being implicated. Age, sex, physical
and mental abnormalities, loyalty, revenge, social and economic
status, indulgence in alcohol, and the influence of other persons
are some of the many factors which may affect the accuracy, willing-
ness, or ability with which witnesses observe, interpret, and
describe occurrences.*

3. According to the above paragraph, a witness may, for       3.___
   personal reasons, give wrong information about an
   occurrence because he
   A. wants to protect his reputation for truthfulness
   B. wants to embarrass the investigator
   C. doesn't want to become involved
   D. doesn't really remember what happened

4. According to the above paragraph, factors which influence   4.___
   the witness of an occurrence may affect
   A. not only what he tells about it, but what he was able
      and wanted to see of it
   B. only what he describes and interprets later but not
      what he actually sees at the time of the event
   C. what he sees but not what he describes
   D. what he is willing to see but not what he is able to see

5. There are few individuals or organizations on whom some     5.___
   records are not kept.
   This sentence means MOST NEARLY that
   A. a few organizations keep most of the records on
      individuals
   B. some of the records on a few individuals are destroyed
      and not kept
   C. there are few records kept on individuals
   D. there is some kind of record kept on almost every
      individual

Questions 6-10.

DIRECTIONS:   Questions 6 through 10 are based SOLELY on the
              following paragraph.

*Those statutes of limitations which are of interest to a claim
examiner are the ones affecting third party actions brought against
an insured covered by a liability policy of insurance. Such statutes
of limitations are legislative enactments limiting the time within
which such actions at law may be brought. Research shows that such
periods differ from state to state and vary within the states with
the type of action brought. The laws of the jurisdiction in which
the action is brought govern and determine the period within which
the action may be instituted, regardless of the place of the cause
of action or the residence of the parties at the time of cause of
action. The period of time set by a statute of limitations for a
tort action starts from the moment the alleged tort is committed.
The period usually extends continuously until its expiration, upon
which legal action may no longer be brought. However, there is a
suspension of the running of the period when a defendant has con-
cealed himself in order to avoid service of legal process. The
suspension continues until the defendant discontinues his concealment and then the period starts running again. A defendant may, by
his agreement or conduct, be legally barred from asserting the
statute of limitations as a defense to an action. The insurance
carrier for the defendant may, by the misrepresentation of the claims
man, cause such a bar against use of the statute of limitations by*

*the defendant. If the claim examiner of the insurance carrier has by his conduct or assertion lulled the plaintiff into a false sense of security by false representations, the defendant may be barred from setting up the statute of limitations as a defense.*

6. Of the following, the MOST suitable title for the above      6.___
   paragraph is
   A. Fraudulent Use of the Statute of Limitations
   B. Parties at Interest in a Lawsuit
   C. The Claim Examiner and the Law
   D. The Statute of Limitations in Claims Work

7. The period of time during which a third party action may be   7.___
   brought against an insured covered by a liability policy
   depends on
   A. the laws of the jurisdiction in which the action is
      brought
   B. where the cause of action which is the subject of the
      suit took place
   C. where the claimant lived at the time of the cause of
      action
   D. where the insured lived at the time of the cause of
      action

8. Time limits in third party actions which are set by the      8.___
   statutes of limitations described above are
   A. determined by claimant's place of residence at start
      of action
   B. different in a state for different actions
   C. the same from state to state for the same type of
      action
   D. the same within a state regardless of type of action

9. According to the above paragraph, grounds which may be        9.___
   legally used to prevent a defendant from using the statute
   of limitations as a defense in the action described are
   A. defendant's agreement or concealment; a charge of
      liability for death and injury
   B. defendant's agreement or conduct; misrepresentation
      by the claims man
   C. fraudulent concealment by claim examiner; a charge of
      liability for death or injury; defendant's agreement
   D. misrepresentation by claim examiner of carrier;
      defendant's agreement; plaintiff's concealment

10. Suppose an alleged tort was committed on January 1, 1985     10.___
    and that the period in which action may be taken is set
    at three years by the statute of limitations. Suppose
    further that the defendant, in order to avoid service of
    legal process, had concealed himself from July 1, 1987
    through December 31, 1987.
    In this case, the defendant may NOT use the statute of
    limitations as a defense unless action is brought by the
    plaintiff after
    A. January 1, 1988        B. February 28, 1988
    C. June 30, 1988          D. August 1, 1988

Questions 11-15.

DIRECTIONS:   Questions 11 through 15 are based SOLELY on the
              information given in the following paragraph.

*The nature of the interview varies with the aim or the use to
which it is put.  While these uses vary widely, interviews are
basically of three types:  fact-finding, informing, and motivating.
One of these purposes usually predominates in an interview, but not
the exclusion of the other two.  If the main purpose is fact-finding,
for example, the interviewer must often motivate the interviewee to
cooperate in revealing the facts.  A major factor in the interview
is the interaction of the personalities of the interviewer and the
interviewee.  The interviewee may not wish to reveal the facts
sought, or even though willing enough to impart them, he may not be
able to do so because of a lack of clear understanding as to what is
wanted or because of lack of ability to put into words the information
he has to give.  On the other hand, the interviewer may not be able
to grasp and report accurately the facts which the one being interviewed is trying to convey.  Also, the interviewer's prejudice may
make him not want to get at the real facts or make him unable to
recognize the truth.*

11.   According to the above paragraph, the purpose of an inter-   11.___
      view
         A. determines the nature of the interview
         B. is usually the same for the three basic types of
            interviews
         C. is predominantly motivation of the interviewee
         D. is usually to check on the accuracy of facts
            previously obtained

12.   In discussing the use or purpose of an interview, the        12.___
      above paragraph points out that
         A. a good interview should have only one purpose
         B. an interview usually has several uses that are equally
            important
         C. fact-finding should be the main purpose of an interview
         D. the interview usually has one main purpose

13.   According to the above paragraph, an obstacle to the         13.___
      successful interview sometimes attributable to the
      interviewee is
         A. a lack of understanding of how to conduct an interview
         B. an inability to express himself
         C. prejudice toward the interviewer
         D. too great a desire to please

14.   According to the above paragraph, one way in which the       14.___
      interviewer may help the interviewee to reveal the facts
      sought is to
         A. make him willing to impart the facts by stating clearly
            the consequences of false information
         B. make sure he understands what information is wanted
         C. motivate him by telling him how important he is in the
            investigation
         D. tell him what words to use to convey the information
            wanted

15. According to the above paragraph, bias on the part of    15.____
the interviewer could
    A. be due to inability to understand the facts being
       imparted
    B. lead him to report the facts accurately
    C. make the interviewee unwilling to impart the truth
    D. prevent him from determining the facts

Questions 16-20.

DIRECTIONS: Questions 16 through 20 are to be based SOLELY on
            the information given in the following paragraph.

*PROCEDURE TO OBTAIN REIMBURSEMENT FROM DEPARTMENT OF HEALTH
FOR CARE OF PHYSICALLY HANDICAPPED CHILDREN*

*Application for reimbursement must be received by the Department
of Health within 30 days of the date of hospital admission in order
that the Department of Hospitals may be reimbursed from the date of
admission. Upon determination that the patient is physically handicapped,
as defined under Chapter 780 of the State Laws, the ward clerk shall
prepare seven copies of Department of Health Form A-1 or A-2 "Application and Authorization," and shall submit six copies to the institutional Collections Unit. The ward clerk shall also initiate two
copies of Department of Health Form B-1 or B-2 "Financial and Social
Report," and shall forward them to the institutional Collections Unit
for completion of page 1 and routing to the Social Service Division
for completion of the Social Summary on page 2. Social Service
Division shall return Form B-1 or B-2 to the institutional Collections
Unit, which shall forward one copy of Form B-1 or B-2 and six copies
of Form A-1 or A-2 to Central Office Division of Collections for
transmission to Bureau of Handicapped Children, Department of Health.*

16. According to the above paragraph, the Department of Health   16.____
will pay for hospital care for
    A. children who are physically handicapped
    B. any children who are ward patients
    C. physically handicapped adults and children
    D. thirty days for eligible children

17. According to the procedure described in the above para-   17.____
graph, the definition of what constitutes a physical
handicap is made by the
    A. attending physician     B. laws of the state
    C. Social Service Division   D. ward clerk

18. According to the above paragraph, Form B-1 or B-2 is   18.____
    A. a three page form containing detachable pages
    B. an authorization form issued by the Department of
       Hospitals
    C. completed by the ward clerk after the Social Summary
       has been entered
    D. sent to the institutional Collections Unit by the
       Social Service Division

19. According to the above paragraph, after their return by         19.___
    the Social Service Division, the institutional Collections
    Unit keeps
    A. one copy of Form A-1 or A-2
    B. one copy of Form A-1 or A-2 and one copy of Form B-1
       or B-2
    C. one copy of Form B-1 or B-2
    D. no copies of Forms A-1 or A-2 or B-1 or B-2

20. According to the above paragraph, forwarding the "Applica-   20.___
    tion and Authorization" to the Department of Health is
    the responsibility of the
    A. Bureau for Handicapped Children
    B. Central Office Division of Collections
    C. Institutional Collections Unit
    D. Social Service Division

21. An investigator interviews members of the public at his     21.___
    desk.
    The attitude of the public toward this department will
    probably be LEAST affected by this investigator's
    A. courtesy   B. efficiency  C. height       D. neatness

22. While you are conducting an interview, the telephone on    22.___
    your desk rings.
    Of the following, it would be BEST for you to
    A. ask the interviewer at the next desk to answer your
       telephone and take the message for you
    B. excuse yourself, pick up the telephone, and tell the
       person on the other end you are busy and will call him
       back later
    C. ignore the ringing telephone and continue with the
       interview
    D. use another telephone to inform the operator not to
       put calls through to you while you are conducting an
       interview

23. An interviewee is at your desk, which is quite near to     23.___
    desks where other people work.  He beckons you a little
    closer and starts to talk in a low voice as though he
    does not want anyone else to hear him.
    Under these circumstances, the BEST thing for you to do
    is to
    A. ask him to speak a little louder so that he can be
       heard
    B. cut the interview short and not get involved in his
       problems
    C. explain that people at other desks are not eavesdroppers
    D. listen carefully to what he says and give it considera-
       tion

24. In the course of your work, you have developed a good      24.____
    relationship with the clerk in charge of the information
    section of a certain government agency from which you must
    frequently obtain information. This agency's procedures
    require that a number of long complicated forms be prepared
    by you before the information can be released.
    For you to ask the clerk in charge to release information
    to you without your presenting the forms would be
      A. *unwise* mainly because the information so obtained is
         no longer considered official
      B. *wise* mainly because a great deal of time will be
         saved by you and by the clerk
      C. *unwise* mainly because it may impair the good relations
         you have established
      D. *wise* mainly because more information can usually be
         obtained through friendly contacts

25. Sometimes city employees are offered gifts by members of    25.____
    the public in an effort to show appreciation for acts
    performed purely as a matter of duty. An investigator
    to whom such a gift was offered refused to accept it.
    The action of the investigator was
      A. *bad*; the gift should have been accepted to avoid being
         rude to the person making the offer
      B. *bad*; salaries paid city employees are not high enough
         to justify such refusals
      C. *good*; he should accept such a gift only when he has
         done a special favor for someone
      D. *good*; the acceptance of such gifts may raise doubts
         as to the honesty of the employee

26. From the point of view of current correct English usage      26.____
    and grammar, the MOST acceptable of the following
    sentences is:
      A. Each claimant was allowed the full amount of their
         medical expenses
      B. Either of the three witnesses is available
      C. Every one of the witnesses was asked to tell his story
      D. Neither of the witnesses are right

27. From the point of view of current correct English usage      27.____
    and grammar, the MOST acceptable of the following
    sentences is:
      A. Beside the statement to the police, the witness spoke
         to no one
      B. He made no statement other than to the police and I
      C. He made no statement to any one else, aside from the
         police
      D. The witness spoke to no one but me

28. From the point of view of current correct English usage      28.____
    and grammar, the MOST acceptable of the following
    sentences is:
      A. The claimant has no one to blame but himself
      B. The boss sent us, he and I, to deliver the packages
      C. The lights come from mine and not his car
      D. There was room on the stairs for him and myself

29. Of the following excerpts selected from letters, the one     29.___
    which is considered by modern letter writing experts to
    be the BEST is:
    A. Attached please find the application form to be filled
       out by you. Return the form to this office at the
       above address.
    B. Forward to this office your check accompanied by the
       application form enclosed with this letter
    C. If you wish to apply, please complete and return the
       enclosed form with your check
    D. In reply to your letter of December ___, enclosed
       herewith please find the application form you requested

30. Which of the following sentences would be MOST acceptable,   30.___
    from the point of view of current correct English usage
    and grammar, in a letter answering a request for information
    about eligibility for clinic care?
    A. Admission to this clinic is limited to patients'
       inability to pay for medical care.
    B. Patients who can pay little or nothing for medical
       care are treated in this clinic.
    C. The patient's ability to pay for medical care is the
       determining factor in his admissibility to this clinic.
    D. This clinic is for the patient's that cannot afford to
       pay or that can pay a little for medical care.

31. A city employee who writes a letter requesting information  31.___
    from a business man should realize that, of the following,
    it is MOST important to
    A. end the letter with a polite closing
    B. make the letter short enough to fit on one page
    C. use a form, such as a questionnaire, to save the
       businessman's time
    D. use a courteous tone that will get the desired
       cooperation

Questions 32-35.

DIRECTIONS:   Each of Questions 32 through 35 consists of a sentence
which may be classified appropriately under one of the
following four categories:
    A. incorrect because of faulty grammar or sentence
       structure
    B. incorrect because of faulty punctuation
    C. incorrect because of faulty capitalization
    D. correct
Examine each sentence carefully. Then, in the space at
the right, print the letter preceding the category which
is the BEST of the four suggested above. Each incorrect
sentence contains only one type of error. Consider a
sentence correct if it contains none of the types of
errors mentioned, although there may be other correct
ways of expressing the same thought.

32. Despite the efforts of the Supervising mechanic, the     32.___
    elevator could not be started.

33. The U.S. Weather Bureau, weather record for the accident    33.___
    date was checked.

34. John Jones accidentally pushed the wrong button and then    34.___
    all the lights went out.

35. The investigator ought to of had the witness sign the       35.___
    statement.

Questions 36-55.

DIRECTIONS:    Each of Questions 36 to 55 consists of a capitalized
               word followed by four suggested meanings of the word.
               For each question, choose the word or phrase which
               means MOST NEARLY the same as the word in capital letters.

36.  ABUT                                                        36.___
     A. abandon      B. assist      C. border on    D. renounce

37.  ABSCOND                                                     37.___
     A. draw in                   B. give up
     C. refrain from              D. steal off

38.  BEQUEATH                                                    38.___
     A. deaden      B. hand down   C. make sad     D. scold

39.  BOGUS                                                       39.___
     A. sad         B. false       C. shocking     D. stolen

40.  CALAMITY                                                    40.___
     A. disaster    B. female      C. insanity     D. patriot

41.  COMPULSORY                                                  41.___
     A. binding     B. ordinary    C. protected    D. ruling

42.  CONSIGN                                                     42.___
     A. agree with  B. benefit     C. commit       D. drive down

43.  DEBILITY                                                    43.___
     A. failure     B. legality    C. quality      D. weakness

44.  DEFRAUD                                                     44.___
     A. cheat       B. deny        C. reveal       D. tie

45.  DEPOSITION                                                  45.___
     A. absence     B. publication C. removal      D. testimony

46.  DOMICILE                                                    46.___
     A. anger       B. dwelling    C. tame         D. willing

47.  HEARSAY                                                     47.___
     A. selfish     B. serious     C. rumor        D. unlikely

48.  HOMOGENEOUS                                                 48.___
     A. human       B. racial      C. similar      D. unwise

49. ILLICIT                                                              49.____
    A. understood  B. uneven       C. unkind      D. unlawful

50. LEDGER                                                               50.____
    A. book of accounts          B. editor
    C. periodical                D. shelf

51. NARRATIVE                                                            51.____
    A. gossip      B. natural     C. negative    D. story

52. PLAUSIBLE                                                            52.____
    A. reasonable                B. respectful
    C. responsible               D. rightful

53. RECIPIENT                                                            53.____
    A. absentee    B. receiver    C. speaker     D. substitute

54. SUBSTANTIATE                                                         54.____
    A. appear for  B. arrange     C. confirm     D. combine

55. SURMISE                                                              55.____
    A. aim         B. break       C. guess       D. order

Questions 56-60.

DIRECTIONS:  In Questions 56 to 60, one of the four words is
             misspelled.  For each question, choose the word
             which is misspelled.

56. A. absence                   B. accummulate                         56.____
    C. acknowledgment            D. audible

57. A. benificiary               B. disbursement                        57.____
    C. exorbitant                D. incidentally

58. A. inoculate   B. liaison    C. acquire     D. noticable            58.____

59. A. peddler     B. permissible C. persuade   D. pertenant            59.____

60. A. reconciliation            B. responsable                         60.____
    C. sizable                   D. substantial

61. Suppose a badly cracked sidewalk, 160 feet long and 14              61.____
    feet wide, is to be torn up and replaced in four equal
    sections.
    Each section will measure ____ square feet.
    A. 40          B. 220         C. 560         D. 680

62. A businessman pays R dollars a month in rent, has a weekly          62.____
    payroll of P dollars, and a utility bill of U dollars for
    each two months.
    His annual expenses can be expressed by
    A. 12(R+P+U)                 B. 52(R+P+U)
    C. 12(R+52P+6U)              D. 12(R+4P+2U)

63. An interviewer can interview P number of people in H number of hours, including the time needed to prepare a report on each interview.
The number of people he can interview in a work week of W hours is represented by

   A. $\dfrac{HW}{P}$       B. $\dfrac{PW}{H}$       C. $\dfrac{PH}{W}$       D. $\dfrac{35H}{P}$

63.____

64. Claims investigated by a certain unit total $8,430,000 for the year.
If the cost of investigating these claims is 17.3 cents per $100, the yearly cost of investigating these claims is MOST NEARLY

   A. $1,450       B. $14,500       C. $145,000       D. $1,450,000

64.____

65. Suppose that a business you are investigating presents the following figures:

| Year | Net Income | Tax Rate on Net Income |
|------|-----------|------------------------|
| 1984 | $55,000 | 20% |
| 1985 | 55,000 | 30% |
| 1986 | 65,000 | 20% |
| 1987 | 52,000 | 25% |
| 1988 | 62,000 | 30% |
| 1989 | 68,000 | 25% |

According to these figures, it is MOST accurate to say that
   A. less tax was due in 1988 than in 1989
   B. more tax was due in 1984 than in 1987
   C. the same amount of tax was due in 1984 and 1985
   D. the same amount of tax was due in 1986 and 1987

65.____

66. In 1986, the number of investigations completed in a certain unit had increased 230 over the number completed in 1985, an increase of 10%. In 1987, the number completed decreased 10% from the number completed in 1986.
Therefore, the number of investigations completed in 1987 was ____ the number completed in 1985.
   A. 23 less than            B. 123 less than
   C. 230 more than           D. the same as

66.____

67. Assume that during a certain period Unit A investigated 400 cases and Unit B investigated 300 cases.
If each unit doubled its number of investigations, the proportion of Unit A's investigations to Unit B's investigations would then be ____ it was.
   A. twice what              B. one-half as large as
   C. one-third larger than   D. the same as

67.____

68. In a certain family, the teenage daughter's annual earnings are 5/8 the earnings of her brother and 1/5 the earnings of her father.
If her brother earns $19,200 a year, then her father's annual earnings are
   A. $60,000       B. $75,000       C. $80,000       D. $96,000

68.____

69. Assume that of the 1,700 verifications made by a certain     69.___
investigating unit in a one week period, 40% were birth
records, 30% were military records, 10% were citizenship
records, and the remainder were miscellaneous records.
Then the MOST accurate of the following statements about
the relative number of different records is that
    A. citizenship records verifications equaled 20% of
       military record verifications
    B. fewer than 700 verifications were birth records
    C. miscellaneous records verifications were 20% more
       than citizenship records verifications
    D. more than 550 verifications were military records

70. Two units, A and B, answer, respectively, 1,000 and 1,500    70.___
inquiries a month.
Assuming that the number of inquiries answered by Unit A
increase at the rate of 20 each month, while those answered
by Unit B decrease at the rate of 5 each month, the two
units will answer the same number of inquiries at the end
of ____ months.
    A. 10          B. 15          C. 20          D. 25

71. For the claim examiner to obtain a signed statement the      71.___
very first time he interviews a witness to an accident
is USUALLY
    A. *bad*; the witness should be given more time in which
       to recall the details of the accident
    B. *good*; delay might result in the witness forgetting
       details
    C. *good*; no further appointments with the witness would
       then be needed
    D. *good*; the story given by this witness would then be
       the first description of the accident

Questions 72-75.

DIRECTIONS:     Questions 72 to 75 are based on the following
                description by a physician of the injuries sustained
                by the victim of an accident.

*Compound fracture of the right humerus. Contusions and*
*ecchymoses of the right chest. Four-inch long laceration on*
*the dorsal surface of the right hand.*

72. According to this description, the victim has a broken       72.___
    A. ankle       B. arm         C. knee        D. thigh

73. The broken bone is                                           73.___
    A. broken in more than one place
    B. crushed
    C. protruding through the skin
    D. splintered

74. Contusions are                                               74.___
    A. bruises              B. skin scrapes or cuts
    C. swellings           D. torn muscles

75. The laceration of the right hand is on the 75.____
    A. back of the hand        B. little finger side
    C. palm                    D. thumb side

76. Suppose a claim examiner desires to obtain a signed 76.____
    statement during an appointment in a witness's home.  He
    finds that the witness is cooperative, but has a large
    family whose members stay with him in the living room,
    talking and looking at television.
    After considering the problem of getting the signed state-
    ment, the claim examiner should
    A. leave after making another appointment since his visit
       is an intrusion at this time
    B. suggest that he and the witness use another room where
       they can give the statement their full attention
    C. take advantage of the friendly atmosphere in the living
       room by having the statement drawn up and signed there
    D. tell the witness to get his family to stop talking and
       to turn off the television set so that he and the
       witness can concentrate

77. Claim examiners occasionally expose fake automobile 77.____
    injury claims in which bruises and lacerations from falls,
    barroom brawls, or other mishaps are attributed to an
    insured commercial vehicle.
    Since the claimant usually tries to pick a situation in
    which the driver is likely to be unaware of the accident
    and so can not contradict the claim, which of the following
    is MOST likely to be the claimant's story?
    A. The front end of a truck with defective brake struck
       him and the truck kept going.
    B. The front end of a truck sideswiped him as the driver
       backed into a parking space.
    C. A truck knocked him over while backing into a loading
       space.
    D. The rear end of a truck making a sharp turn struck him.

78. Suppose there is a rule in your office that signed state- 78.____
    ments of claimants should be witnessed by a person who has
    no direct interest in the claim.
    In accordance with this rule, when a claimant is willing
    to sign a statement in his home, it would be BEST for you
    to have the claimant's signature witnessed by
    A. a neighbor              B. his attorney
    C. his wife                D. yourself

79. The attitude presented by the claim examiner to the 79.____
    claimant should ALWAYS leave the claimant with the feeling
    that
    A. he will be treated fairly
    B. he will receive damages
    C. his claim has no basis
    D. the claim examiner is his friend

80. If a claimant states that his vision has been impaired       80.____
    by an accident, it would be BEST to have him examined
    by a physician who is a specialist in
    A. dermatology              B. opthalmology
    C. otology                  D. urology

81. Suppose that witness W tells you, the claim examiner, that   81.____
    Mr. X also witnessed the accident you are investigating.
    Mr. X denies that he has any knowledge of the accident.
    For you to have Mr. X sign a statement that he has no
    knowledge of the accident is wise MAINLY because such a
    statement
    A. casts doubt on Mr. X's reliability if he should be a
       surprise witness for the opposition
    B. makes it unnecessary for you to further investigate
       Mr. X
    C. proves that Mr. X is telling the truth
    D. proves that the statements made by witness W are
       unreliable and should be investigated further

82. A claim examiner admitted that the settlement negotiations   82.____
    were not progressing because of a clash of personalities
    and suggested that another claim examiner continue the
    negotiations.
    Such an action by the claim examiner is
    A. *sensible*; it reduces his responsibility if the
       settlement negotiations fail
    B. *foolish*; it is an admission that he has an irritating
       personality and can not get along with people
    C. *sensible*; it shows he recognizes the problem and a
       possible method of completing the settlement
    D. *foolish*; it gives the claimant an advantage in the
       negotiations

83. In evaluating a doctor's fitness to serve as an expert       83.____
    witness in a negligence case, the claim examiner should
    give FIRST consideration to the doctor's
    A. field of specialization
    B. previous total experience as a witness in negligence
       cases
    C. standing in the community and in his profession
    D. total formal schooling

84. A claim examiner, showing his identification, introduced     84.____
    himself to a housewife by saying, *I am Mr. Nichols from the
    Department of ....... We are trying to get information
    about an accident which occurred in front of your house.*
    The claim examiner's approach was
    A. *good*; by identifying himself and stating his purpose,
       he is apt to get better cooperation
    B. *good*; by giving his name, he puts the interview on a
       non-personal basis
    C. *poor*; by revealing his purpose immediately, he may lose
       the woman's cooperation because of fear
    D. *poor*; he should stress the importance of cooperating
       with city departments

85. Witness A describes an individual as being *of medium height*. Witness B describes the same individual as being *tall and thin*.
To clear up this difference in description of the individual's height, it would be BEST for you to
   A. ask another witness to describe the individual
   B. ask both witnesses to compare the individual's height with that of a person of known height
   C. average the difference and describe the individual as being *medium tall*
   D. check both witnesses' judgment on other factors to decide which witness is more reliable

85.____

86. A claimant against the city is in the hospital as the result of an automobile accident. An interview with this claimant might eliminate confusion caused by contradictory statements of witnesses to the accident.
Under these circumstances, the BEST action for the claim examiner assigned to the case to take FIRST is to
   A. determine whether the claimant is in a condition that would permit an interview
   B. postpone interviewing the claimant until he leaves the hospital
   C. try to resolve the problem by re-examining the witnesses whose statements are in conflict
   D. try to get an immediate short interview in case the person should die

86.____

87. The claimant is an occupant of a building, ownership of which was taken over by the city one day before his accident. He has bruises and contusions which he attributes to tripping on a loose board on a stairway. Several tenants state that they had complained many times to the previous owner of the building about the same loose board.
Which of the following would tend MOST to suggest fraudulent intent on the part of the claimant?
   A. The claimant is represented by an insurance company with which he holds a policy covering this type of accident.
   B. The claimant is the previous owner of the building, and there are no witnesses to the accident.
   C. It is established by reliable witnesses that the claimant tripped over the loose board while intoxicated.
   D. Witnesses state that the claimant tripped over the loose board while chasing a stray dog down the stairway.

87.____

88. At the request of the investigator, witness A added a signed paragraph to a statement already signed by witness B while witness B was present. This paragraph stated that witness A's version of the accident was exactly the same as that of witness B.
Authorities in the field of claim examining would GENERALLY consider the addition of such a paragraph as
   A. *good*; it makes the statement of witness B more believable
   B. *bad*; witness A should have been asked to add his statement after witness B had left

88.____

C. *good*; the effect is to make both witnesses more cooperative

D. *bad*; since witnesses rarely give identical versions of an accident, the validity of this additional statement would be questioned

89. The motorman's statement was that he had applied brakes immediately on seeing the man collapse and fall onto the tracks, but he could not stop soon enough and ran over him.

If proving absence of negligence in this case depends entirely on showing that the accident was beyond the motorman's control, which of the following circumstances would, by itself, show that there was no negligence?

A. Five witnesses agreed independently that the man had apparently collapsed from a heart attack.

B. Five witnesses agreed independently that the train was traveling at a speed which was far under the normal approach speed.

C. The motorman's record showed that he had been involved in no previous accident although employed thirty years as a motorman.

D. At the moment the man fell, the distance between him and the train was less than the minimum distance at which the train could stop at normal approach speed.

90. No proper evaluation of a claim can be made without a working knowledge of the law of the jurisdiction in which an accident occurred.

Of the following, the CHIEF implication of this statement is that

A. claims are based on where the accident occurred

B. evaluation of the law is a proper function of the claim examiner

C. local laws affect the claim examiner's decisions

D. the best claim examiners are attorneys

# KEY (CORRECT ANSWERS)

| | | | | | |
|---|---|---|---|---|---|
| 1. | A | 31. | D | 61. | C |
| 2. | B | 32. | C | 62. | C |
| 3. | C | 33. | B | 63. | B |
| 4. | A | 34. | D | 64. | B |
| 5. | D | 35. | A | 65. | D |
| | | | | | |
| 6. | D | 36. | C | 66. | A |
| 7. | A | 37. | D | 67. | D |
| 8. | B | 38. | B | 68. | A |
| 9. | B | 39. | B | 69. | B |
| 10. | C | 40. | A | 70. | C |
| | | | | | |
| 11. | A | 41. | A | 71. | B |
| 12. | D | 42. | C | 72. | D |
| 13. | B | 43. | D | 73. | C |
| 14. | B | 44. | A | 74. | A |
| 15. | D | 45. | D | 75. | A |
| | | | | | |
| 16. | A | 46. | B | 76. | B |
| 17. | B | 47. | C | 77. | D |
| 18. | D | 48. | C | 78. | A |
| 19. | C | 49. | D | 79. | A |
| 20. | B | 50. | A | 80. | B |
| | | | | | |
| 21. | C | 51. | D | 81. | A |
| 22. | B | 52. | A | 82. | C |
| 23. | D | 53. | B | 83. | A |
| 24. | C | 54. | C | 84. | A |
| 25. | D | 55. | C | 85. | B |
| | | | | | |
| 26. | C | 56. | B | 86. | A |
| 27. | D | 57. | A | 87. | B |
| 28. | A | 58. | D | 88. | D |
| 29. | C | 59. | D | 89. | D |
| 30. | B | 60. | B | 90. | C |

# EXAMINATION SECTION

DIRECTIONS: Each question or incomplete statement is followed by several suggested answers or completions. Select the one that BEST answers the question or completes the statement. *PRINT THE LETTER OF THE CORRECT ANSWER IN THE SPACE AT THE RIGHT.*

1. It is desirable for an examiner to keep a regular periodic check on witnesses for the city in a negligence suit MAINLY because, in this way, he can
   A. coach the witnesses thoroughly on the testimony they are to give
   B. develop new leads to previously unknown sources of information
   C. lessen the chance of losing track of witnesses before the suit goes to trial
   D. show these witnesses how important they are to the city's case

1.___

2. A certain examiner follows the practice of having the claimant or his attorney place a settlement value on their claim before he makes any settlement offer himself. Such a practice is GENERALLY
   A. *desirable* because the claimant will realize that his interests are being given consideration by the examiner
   B. *undesirable* because it leads to delays in settlements by encouraging differences between claims and offers
   C. *desirable* because the demand made by the claimant or his attorney may show the examiner that he has over-valued the claim
   D. *undesirable* because the claimant and attorney will always set a high settlement figure

2.___

3. The preliminary investigation of a fatal subway accident reveals that the wife of the victim took out a large insurance policy on his life shortly before the accident. In evaluating this information, the examiner should realize that it
   A. is important enough to warrant further investigation
   B. is important evidence of the criminal involvement of the wife
   C. is purely coincidental and no special significance should be attached to it
   D. points strongly to the probability of suicide

3.___

4. In a vehicle collision case involving a city vehicle and a privately-owned vehicle legally parked at the curb, the driver of the city vehicle admitted to the examiner for the city that the accident was entirely his fault. The action of the city driver in admitting blame for the accident should

4.___

   A. *be* criticized; it will encourage the claimant in his
      suit against the city
   B. *not be* criticized; it will influence the claimant to
      make a more reasonable settlement demand against the
      city
   C. *be* criticized; the question of liability must be
      decided by a competent court of law
   D. *not be* criticized; liability is clear-cut in view of
      the conditions that existed at the time of the
      accident

5. Of the following, the CHIEF objective of the examiner who       5.___
   investigates an automobile accident claim should be to
   A. complete his investigation in the shortest possible
      time while the memory of the event is still fresh
   B. get the facts for use as evidence in court or as a
      basis for settlement
   C. steer the claimant toward accepting a settlement of
      the claim
   D. try to lay a basis for disproving the liability of
      the city

6. In law, the rule of negligence provides that to hold a          6.___
   person liable for another's injury, there must have been
   a duty owed by the former to the latter.
   The duty MOST probably referred to in the preceding state-
   ment is the duty to
   A. advise regarding the possible consequences of the
      action contemplated
   B. exercise reasonable care to prevent the injury
   C. provide speedy medical assistance when needed
   D. refuse entry into the vehicle or the premises

7. Claimants and witnesses become suspicious when the              7.___
   examiner makes a *callback* to get additional information
   which he should have obtained in the initial contact.
   Of the following, the CHIEF implication of this statement
   for the examiner in his work is that he should
   A. carefully plan the *callback* interview in such a way
      as to avoid arousing suspicions of claimants and
      witnesses
   B. frankly state the reason for the *callback* to the
      claimant or witness so that suspicions will be allayed
   C. not make any *callbacks* in order not to arouse the
      suspicions of claimants and witnesses
   D. thoroughly plan his initial interview so as to obtain
      complete and correct information and avoid the need
      for *callback*

8. It is desirable for an examiner to be familiar with             8.___
   medical terminology relating to bodily injuries MAINLY
   because this familiarity will
   A. assist him in determining whether a claimant is
      being given proper care

B. enable him to determine whether a claimant's injuries have been fully and properly described on the hospital records
C. give him a sympathetic approach to discussing a claim with the injured person
D. help him understand medical reports that he may refer to in the course of the investigation of a claim

9. Assume that a city vehicle is forced to stop short by another vehicle in front of it. As a result, a third vehicle runs into the rear of the city vehicle. The driver of the third vehicle files a claim against the city alleging that the city vehicle's short stop caused the accident.
The examiner assigned to this case should recommend
   A. denial of the claim since the rear vehicle in such a situation should be at a sufficient distance to stop in time
   B. settling the claim since the city vehicle is the direct cause of the actual collision
   C. denial of this claim since the real cause of the accident is the first vehicle's improper stop
   D. settling the claim but bringing in the driver of the first vehicle as the defendant liable for all the damage

9.___

10. The investigating staff of the Department of Hospitals often processes liability claims for accident victims who are hospitalized in municipal hospitals.
Of the following, the MOST probable reason why the investigating staff processes such claims is that
   A. reimbursement of the hospital for the victim's care may be facilitated by such action
   B. such action is required by and consistent with the effort to reduce the number of accidents in the city
   C. the processing of such liability claims requires little effort and results in better public relations
   D. the welfare of the patient is usually considered above everything else

10.___

11. Suppose that, as a matter of policy, insurance company representatives are not permitted to inspect the hospital records of patients without the latter's written consent.
Such a policy is
   A. *justified* because information about a patient's ailment or disease is confidential and private
   B. *unjustified* because nobody should be required to give information about his medical condition
   C. *justified* because these records may be meaningful to a medical person but not to a layman
   D. *unjustified* because such matters should be left to the hospital administrator

11.___

12. Continuous taking of notes during an interview is      12.___
GENERALLY
   A. *desirable* because no important facts will be forgotten
   B. *undesirable* because it gives the person being interviewed a clue to the importance of the information being obtained from him
   C. *desirable* because the interviewer cannot write as fast as the person being interviewed can speak
   D. *undesirable* because it may put the person being interviewed ill at ease

13. In deciding whether to make use of a source of information    13.___
tion in connection with an investigation, the examiner should be influenced MAINLY by the
   A. expense entailed in the use of the source
   B. relative availability of the source
   C. relative proximity of the source
   D. reliability of the information offered by the source

14. An examiner's report always includes his personal judg-    14.___
ment of the credibility of witnesses mentioned in his report.
This practice is
   A. *desirable*, mainly because it can be used to support the position that the examiner wants to take with respect to the case
   B. *undesirable*, mainly because it is of no value to the reader of the report
   C. *desirable*, mainly because it is part of the claim examining function to evaluate the credibility of witnesses
   D. *undesirable*, mainly because judgments should be formed on the basis of facts, not opinions

15. When a statement which may be submitted as evidence in    15.___
court has been secured from a person after questioning, it is often typed up with intentional errors and given to the person to read.
Such action is USUALLY based on a
   A. desire to be able to counteract any later denial by the person that he was aware of the contents; if the person corrects and initials the errors and then signs the statement, it is evidence that he was aware of the contents
   B. desire to distinguish the truthful from the untruthful person; an error which makes for inconsistency within the statement will be noticed much more readily by the truthful person
   C. need for careful proofreading; when the person discovers several mistakes, he will be alerted to watch for other possible mistakes
   D. need for testing the mental functioning of the person at the time of making the statement; if he does not detect the errors, he is functioning abnormally

16. Suppose you are checking an alphabetical card reference       16.\_\_\_
    file to locate information about a *George Dyerly*.  After
    checking all the *D*'s, you can find a card only for a
    *George Dyrely*.
    Of the following, the BEST action for you to take is to
    A. check the balance of the file to see if the card you
       are interested in has been misfiled
    B. check the data on the card to see if it relates to
       the same person in whom you are interested
    C. correct the spelling of the name on your records
       and reports to conform to the spelling on the card
    D. reject this reference file as a source of information
       regarding this person

17. Mary Hartley, age 40, wife of William Hartley, had stated    17.\_\_\_
    in an application that she was a graduate of a certain
    high school and had completed 2 years of college in
    another city.  A written inquiry to these two schools
    brought the reply that they had no record of Mary Hartley
    ever having attended their respective schools.
    Of the following, it is MOST probable that the
    A. records in question, being rather old, had been
       destroyed
    B. records in question had been lost or misplaced
    C. woman exaggerated her education in her application
    D. woman was listed on the school records under
       another name

18. Of the following, the MOST important reason why an examiner   18.\_\_\_
    should maintain a good working relationship with law
    enforcement officers in the community is that
    A. all government employees, whether city, state, or
       federal, should keep in close touch with each other
       in view of their common interests
    B. community law enforcement officers may sometimes
       need the assistance of the examiner in a police
       matter
    C. law enforcement is most effective when all elements
       in the community cooperate
    D. these officers often know a great many facts regard-
       ing the citizens of a community which are not matters
       of public record

19. In fidelity bond investigations, the employer applying        19.\_\_\_
    for the bond is investigated in addition to the employee
    to be bonded.
    The MOST likely reason for this is that
    A. employers can be depended upon to be reliable but
       fraud by an employer involves greater sums of money
    B. the employer's auditing methods and his methods of
       handling valuables affect his risk status
    C. there are as many dishonest employers as there are
       dishonest employees
    D. there is such a great number of cases where the
       employer and the employee conspire to defraud the
       insurance company

20. An examiner who wanted to interview the head of a
business firm introduced himself by saying, *I am James
Smith of the State Legal Department, and I would like
to check with you certain information given us by
Herbert Brown, a former employee of yours.*
The approach used by the examiner was
    A. *good* because by giving so little information, he has
       lost nothing if the employer should refuse to cooper-
       ate
    B. *poor* because he should first try to establish a
       friendly relationship with the employer before stating
       the purpose of his visit
    C. *good* because he came directly to the point by stating
       who he was and what he wanted
    D. *poor* because he should have stressed with the employer
       the importance of cooperating with government agen-
       cies in all investigative matters

20.___

21. The examiner should never rely entirely on the data given
him by a witness.
Of the following, the CHIEF justification for this statement is the fact that
    A. human perceptions are often incomplete and frequently
       affected by distortions
    B. recall and recognition are apt to be more accurate
       when the passage of time has caused momentary passions
       and prejudices to cool
    C. a witness to an occurrence cannot always be found
    D. witnesses usually contradict each other

21.___

22. The first 3 numerals in a social security number indicate
the state where the employee resided when the number was
assigned.
According to the preceding statement, if your investigation indicates that the first 3 numerals of a New York
resident's Social Security number do not correspond to
the numbers for the state, it is MOST reasonable to conclude that
    A. the numbers assigned to New York have been revised
    B. there is an error in the Social Security number
    C. this person at one time did not live in New York
    D. this person is not a bona fide New York resident

22.___

23. The examiner's general plans for the investigation should
be determined before he starts on a case.
Of the following, the BEST argument in favor of this
procedure is that
    A. a plan once adopted should not be modified unless
       there are very good reasons for doing so
    B. steps in the investigation which duplicate each other
       or are of little value will be minimized
    C. the plan for each investigation will be different
    D. until an investigation is actually begun, it is
       difficult to know the problems that will be encountered

23.___

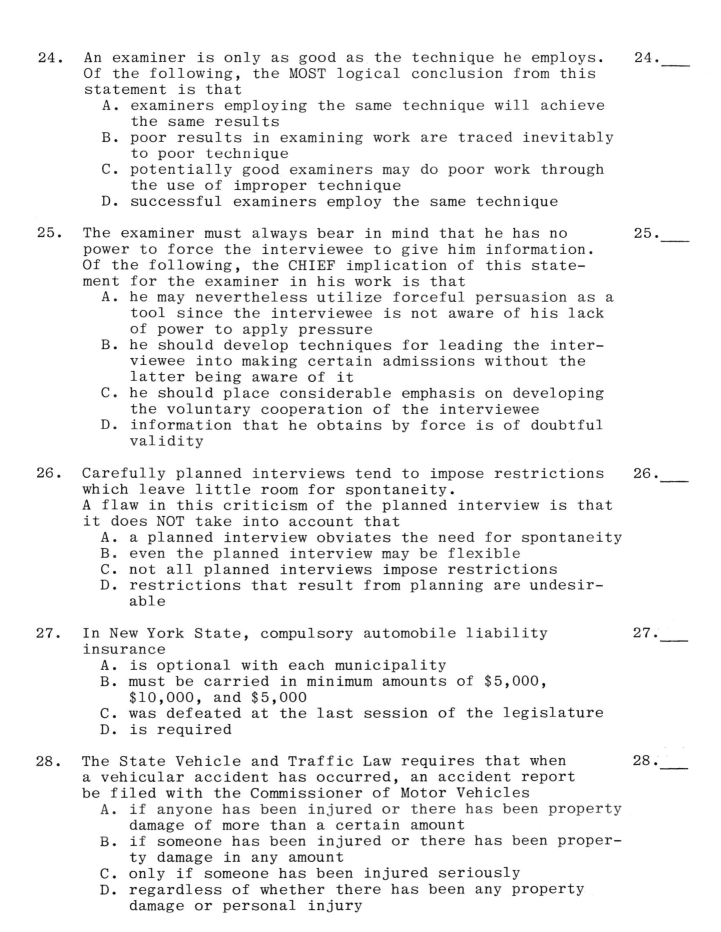

24. An examiner is only as good as the technique he employs.    24.\_\_\_
    Of the following, the MOST logical conclusion from this
    statement is that
    A. examiners employing the same technique will achieve
       the same results
    B. poor results in examining work are traced inevitably
       to poor technique
    C. potentially good examiners may do poor work through
       the use of improper technique
    D. successful examiners employ the same technique

25. The examiner must always bear in mind that he has no    25.\_\_\_
    power to force the interviewee to give him information.
    Of the following, the CHIEF implication of this state-
    ment for the examiner in his work is that
    A. he may nevertheless utilize forceful persuasion as a
       tool since the interviewee is not aware of his lack
       of power to apply pressure
    B. he should develop techniques for leading the inter-
       viewee into making certain admissions without the
       latter being aware of it
    C. he should place considerable emphasis on developing
       the voluntary cooperation of the interviewee
    D. information that he obtains by force is of doubtful
       validity

26. Carefully planned interviews tend to impose restrictions    26.\_\_\_
    which leave little room for spontaneity.
    A flaw in this criticism of the planned interview is that
    it does NOT take into account that
    A. a planned interview obviates the need for spontaneity
    B. even the planned interview may be flexible
    C. not all planned interviews impose restrictions
    D. restrictions that result from planning are undesir-
       able

27. In New York State, compulsory automobile liability    27.\_\_\_
    insurance
    A. is optional with each municipality
    B. must be carried in minimum amounts of $5,000,
       $10,000, and $5,000
    C. was defeated at the last session of the legislature
    D. is required

28. The State Vehicle and Traffic Law requires that when    28.\_\_\_
    a vehicular accident has occurred, an accident report
    be filed with the Commissioner of Motor Vehicles
    A. if anyone has been injured or there has been property
       damage of more than a certain amount
    B. if someone has been injured or there has been proper-
       ty damage in any amount
    C. only if someone has been injured seriously
    D. regardless of whether there has been any property
       damage or personal injury

29. A form relating to possible insurance coverage of accident 29.___
    victims has a space headed *Name of Carrier*.
    The word *carrier* in this case MOST probably refers to the
    A. accident victim          B. insurance company
    C. policy beneficiary       D. policy holder

30. In the business world, title companies are GENERALLY          30.___
    concerned with matters relating to the
    A. investment in securities
    B. laws of copyright
    C. ownership of real property
    D. registration of patents

31. A person who has *derivative* United States citizenship is    31.___
    one who has citizenship through
    A. birth in the United States
    B. his own naturalization proceedings
    C. marriage with a naturalized citizen
    D. the naturalization of a parent

32. As most commonly employed, the term *vital statistics*        32.___
    refers to records of
    A. automobile accidents
    B. births and deaths
    C. crimes known to the police
    D. stock market transactions

Questions 33-35.

DIRECTIONS: Questions 33 through 35 are to be answered SOLELY on the
            basis of the information given in the following statement.

*When a voluntary hospital admits a Blue Cross subscriber who has
been referred from a city hospital, a concurrent submission of the
case shall be made by it to both Blue Cross and the city investigator
who routinely visits the voluntary hospital. This procedure will be
advantageous to both the voluntary hospital and the city since the
hospital would be notified immediately of the ability of the city to
reimburse should Blue Cross coverage be inapplicable or insufficient;
furthermore, the city will be able to assure itself of potential state
aid for those cases for whom it may have to assume some responsibility.
Necessary time limits to process applications for state aid can also
be made if this referral is concurrent, such as for state charges and
relief clients, who are frequently Blue Cross members. This investigation can best be conducted by the city staff assigned to the
voluntary hospital, rather than by the staff in the referring
municipal hospital.*

33. According to the above statement, one responsibility of a     33.___
    voluntary hospital with respect to an admission who is a
    Blue Cross subscriber is to
    A. get the city to reimburse its fair share if Blue
       Cross coverage is inapplicable or insufficient

   B. refer the case to the city hospital for possible
      collection of state aid
   C. submit the case concurrently to both Blue Cross and
      the city investigator
   D. submit the case to the city investigator if the
      patient has been referred by a city hospital

34. According to the above statement, it is NOT an advantage    34.___
    of the procedure described that the
    A. city can make sure of getting possible state aid for
       those cases for whom it may be partly responsible
    B. cost of caring for the cases referred to will be
       shared by Blue Cross, the voluntary hospital, the
       city, and the state
    C. needed time limits to handle state aid applications
       can be made
    D. voluntary hospitals will know immediately if the city
       will pay for its referrals who do not have enough
       Blue Cross coverage

35. According to the above statement, the investigation         35.___
    referred to can be carried out MOST advantageously by
    the
    A. city investigator who routinely visits the voluntary
       hospital
    B. city staff assigned to the hospital that admitted
       the patient
    C. staff of the hospital that referred the patient
    D. staff of the voluntary hospital that accepted the
       referral

36. To have analytical habits and a scientific approach is a    36.___
    necessary qualification for the development of a first-
    rate examiner.  But it is also true that the main source
    of people with such qualifications, the body of scien-
    tists, mathematicians, and logicians who constantly
    advance the state of human knowledge, does not contain
    many people who could be developed into first-rate
    examiners.
    On the basis of this statement, it is MOST reasonable to
    assume that
    A. in order to develop into a very good examiner, a
       person needs something more than analytical habits
       and a scientific approach
    B. examiners should receive intensive training in
       science, mathematics, and logic
    C. most successful examiners are drawn from the fields
       of science, mathematics, and logic
    D. the eccentricities usually found in the behavior of
       scientists, mathematicians, and logicians are not
       conducive to the development of first-rate examiners

37.  A greater variety of accounts of the circumstances of an        37.___
     accident is likely to result when the witnesses are
     interviewed separately than when they are interviewed as
     a group.
     Of the following, the MOST valid inference from this
     statement is that
       A. a truer picture of the circumstances of an accident
          can be obtained through interviewing the witnesses
          as a group than through interviewing them separately
       B. interviewing of accident witnesses individually
          offers a greater chance that individual versions of
          the accident will be obtained than interviewing the
          same witnesses as a group
       C. people who witness an accident as part of a group are
          more likely to agree on the circumstances of the
          accident than those witnesses who are separated at
          the time of the accident and see the accident from
          different angles
       D. witnesses are not as likely to tell the truth when
          they are interviewed privately as when they are inter-
          viewed as a group

Questions 38-39.

DIRECTIONS:  Questions 38 and 39 are to be answered SOLELY on the
             basis of the information given in the following para-
             graph.


     *It is argued by some that the locale of the trial should be
given little or no consideration. Facts are facts, they say; and
if presented properly to a jury panel, they will be productive of
the same results regardless of where the trial is held. However,
experience shows great differences in the methods of handling
claims by juries. In some counties, large demands in personal
injury suits are viewed with suspicion by the jury. In others,
the jurors are liberal in dealing with someone else's funds.*


38.  According to the above paragraph, it would be advisable        38.___
     for an examiner on a personal injury case to
       A. get information as to the kind of verdicts that are
          usually awarded by juries in the county of trial
       B. give little or no consideration to the locale of the
          trial
       C. look for incomplete and improper presentation of
          facts to the jury if the verdict was not justified
          by the facts
       D. offer a high but realistic initial settlement figure
          so that no temptation is left to the claimant to
          gamble on the jury's verdict

39. According to the above statement, the argument that the    39.___
    location of a trial in a personal injury suit CANNOT
    counteract the weight of the evidence is
    A. basically sound
    B. disproven by the differences in awards for similar
       claims
    C. substantiated in those cases where the facts are
       properly and carefully presented to the injury
    D. supported by experience which shows great differences
       in the methods of handling claims by juries

Questions 40-42.

DIRECTIONS:   Questions 40 through 42 are to be answered SOLELY on
              the basis of the information given in the following
              paragraph.

*A loan receipt is an instrument devised to permit the insurance
company to bring an action against the wrongdoer in the name of the
insured despite the fact that the insured no longer has any financial
interest in the outcome. It provides, in effect, that the amount of
the loss is advanced to the insured as a loan which is repayable only
up to the extent of any recovery made from the wrongdoer. The
insured further agrees to enter and prosecute suit against the wrongdoer in his own name. Such a receipt substitutes a loan for a payment
for the purpose of permitting the insurance company to press its
action against the wrongdoer in the name of the insured.*

40. According to the above paragraph, the purpose behind the    40.___
    use of a loan receipt is to
    A. guarantee that the insurance company gets repayment
       from the person insured
    B. insure repayment of all expenditures to the named
       insured
    C. make it possible for the insurance company to sue in
       the name of the policy owner
    D. prevent the wrongdoer from escaping the natural
       consequences of his act

41. According to the above paragraph, the amount of the loan    41.___
    which must be paid back to the insurance company equals
    but does NOT exceed the amount
    A. of the loss
    B. on the face of the policy
    C. paid to the insured
    D. recovered from the wrongdoer

42. According to the above paragraph, by giving a loan          42.___
    receipt, the person insured agrees to
    A. a suit against the wrongdoer in his own name
    B. forego any financial gain from the outcome of the
       suit
    C. institute an action on behalf of the insurance company
    D. repay the insurance company for the loan received

Questions 43-44.

DIRECTIONS: Questions 43 and 44 are to be answered SOLELY on the basis of the information given in the following paragraph.

*Hospitals maintained wholly by public taxation may treat only those compensation cases which are emergencies and may not treat such emergency cases longer than the emergency exists; provided, however, that these restrictions shall not be applicable where there is not available a hospital other than a hospital maintained wholly by taxation.*

43. According to the above paragraph, compensation cases 43.___
    A. are regarded as emergency cases by hospitals main-
       tained wholly by public taxation
    B. are seldom treated by hospitals maintained wholly
       by public taxation
    C. are treated mainly by privately endowed hospitals
    D. may be treated by hospitals maintained wholly by
       public taxation if they are emergencies

44. According to the above paragraph, it is MOST reasonable 44.___
    to conclude that where a privately endowed hospital is
    available
    A. a hospital supported wholly by public taxation may
       treat emergency compensation cases only so long as
       the emergency exists
    B. a hospital supported wholly by public taxation may
       treat any compensation cases
    C. a hospital supported wholly by public taxation must
       refer emergency compensation cases to such a hospital
    D. the restrictions regarding the treatment of compen-
       sation cases by a tax-supported hospital are not
       wholly applicable

Questions 45-46.

DIRECTIONS: Questions 45 and 46 are to be answered SOLELY on the basis of the information given in the following paragraph.

*An assumption commonly made in regard to the reliability of testimony is that when a number of persons report upon the same matter, those details upon which there is an agreement may, in general, be considered as substantiated. Experiments have shown, however, that there is a tendency for the same errors to appear in the testimony of different individuals, and that, quite apart from any collusion, agreement of testimony is no proof of dependability.*

45. According to the above paragraph, it is commonly assumed 45.___
    that details of an event are substantiated when
    A. a number of persons report upon them
    B. a reliable person testifies to them

    C. no errors are apparent in the testimony of different
       individuals
    D. several witnesses are in agreement about them

46. According to the above paragraph, agreement in the testi-   46.___
mony of different witnesses to the same event is
    A. evaluated more reliably when considered apart from
       collusion
    B. not the result of chance
    C. not a guarantee of the accuracy of the facts
    D. the result of a mass reaction of the witnesses

Questions 47-48.

DIRECTIONS:   Questions 47 and 48 are to be answered SOLELY on the
                basis of the information given in the following para-
                graph.

*The accuracy of the information about past occurrence obtainable in an interview is so low that one must take the stand that the best use to be made of the interview in this connection is a means of finding clues and avenues of access to more reliable sources of information. On the other hand, feelings and attitudes have been found to be clearly and correctly revealed in a properly conducted personal interview.*

47. According to the above paragraph, information obtained in   47.___
a personal interview
    A. can be corroborated by other clues and more reliable
       sources of information revealed at the interview
    B. can be used to develop leads to other sources of
       information about past events
    C. is not reliable
    D. is reliable if it relates to recent occurrences

48. According to the above paragraph, the personal interview   48.___
is suitable for obtaining
    A. emotional reactions to a given situation
    B. fresh information on factors which may be forgotten
    C. revived recollection of previous events for later
       use as testimony
    D. specific information on material already reduced to
       writing

49. Even if no one else is interested in the case you are   49.___
investigating, it is still recommended that you keep a
record of the progress of the case by means of regular
reports for the file.
Of the following, the one which is NOT a good reason for
this recommendation is that
    A. it is difficult for the memory to retain all the
       information gathered on every case during the course
       of daily investigations

B. it may become necessary to review the case while the person assigned to it is temporarily away from the office because of illness or other reason
C. the final report on the investigation will be briefer if it includes only the important material from the daily reports
D. the person investigating the case may resign or transfer to another job

50. The most thorough investigation is of no value if the report written by the investigator does not enable the reader to readily decide the correct action to be taken. Of the following, the LEAST direct implication of the preceding paragraph is that the
    A. investigation conducted must be very thorough to be of value
    B. investigation report is generally written by the person who made the investigation
    C. purpose of the investigation report is to give superiors a basis for action
    D. worth of the investigation is affected by the report submitted

50.___

51. Before you submit the written report of an investigation which you conducted, you become aware of some previously unknown information relating to the case.
    Your decision as to whether to rewrite your report to include this additional information should be influenced MAINLY by the
    A. amount of time remaining in which to submit the report
    B. bearing this additional information will have on the findings and recommendations of the report
    C. extent of the revision that will be required in the original report in order to include this additional information
    D. feasibility of submitting a supplementary report at a later date

51.___

52. When dictating a report to a stenographer, it is LEAST important to
    A. be brief and say only what is essential
    B. be emphatic and speak with expression
    C. spell out all involved words
    D. work from an outline previously prepared

52.___

53. When signed statements of witnesses are forwarded with the report of an investigation, it is generally BEST to
    A. merely highlight the main points of the statements in the report, commenting on any contradictions
    B. repeat the statements verbatim in the body of the report and call attention to the original statements attached
    C. retype in the report those parts of the statements that are not significant and of doubtful validity, thus calling the reader's attention to them and avoiding misinterpretation

53.___

D. save space by not taking up the statements in the
   report since they are attached and available to the
   reader of the report

Questions 54-68.

DIRECTIONS:   In each of Questions 54 through 68, select the lettered
              word or phrase which means MOST NEARLY the same as the
              italicized word.

54. *abet*                                                          54.\_\_\_
    A. crush       B. encourage   C. gamble       D. reduce

55. *abeyance*                                                      55.\_\_\_
    A. assistance            B. conclusion
    C. obedience             D. suspension

56. *allege*                                                        56.\_\_\_
    A. affirm      B. increase    C. legalize     D. prove

57. *allusion*                                                      57.\_\_\_
    A. deposit               B. image
    C. impression            D. reference

58. *brevity*                                                       58.\_\_\_
    A. fearless              B. pointless
    C. shortness             D. truthfulness

59. *cognizance*                                                    59.\_\_\_
    A. awareness             B. convincing
    C. soundness             D. timeliness

60. *collusion*                                                     60.\_\_\_
    A. accident              B. deceit
    C. deduction             D. imagination

61. *conjecture*                                                    61.\_\_\_
    A. agreement             B. conjunction
    C. failure               D. guess

62. *defalcation*                                                   62.\_\_\_
    A. absence               B. dying
    C. embezzlement          D. rejection

63. *derogatory*                                                    63.\_\_\_
    A. concealed             B. deserving
    C. detracting            D. questioning

64. *interlocutory*                                                 64.\_\_\_
    A. intermediate          B. prompt
    C. soothing              D. wordy

65. *suborn*                                                    65.___
    A. decorate                 B. distribute
    C. incite                     D. subtract

66. *subrogate*                                                 66.___
    A. legislate               B. remove
    C. substitute            D. support

67. *surety*                                                    67.___
    A. gain     B. guarantee    C. increase   D. spoilage

68. *tort*                                                      68.___
    A. active interest        B. concise
    C. involved interpretation  D. wrongful act

Questions 68-73.

DIRECTIONS:    Each of Questions 68 through 73 consists of four words.
                Three of the words are spelled correctly; one is spelled
                incorrectly.  For each question, select the word that is
                spelled INCORRECTLY.

69. A. collateral            B. possesion       69.___
    C. relevant             D. superficial

70. A. fluorescent         B. maintenance     70.___
    C. occurrence           D. tecnical

71. A. hindrance            B. interval        71.___
    C. liquidate            D. preceeding

72. A. questionnaire       B. superintendant   72.___
    C. temporarily          D. vaccination

73. A. resipient             B. significant     73.___
    C. unanimous           D. variable

74. From the point of view of current correct English usage   74.___
    and grammar, the MOST acceptable of the following
    sentences is:
    A. An agreement was reached between the defendant, the
       plaintiff, the plaintiff's attorney and the insurance
       company as to the amount of the settlement.
    B. Everybody was asked to give their versions of the
       accident.
    C. The consensus of opinion was that the evidence was
       inconclusive.
    D. The witness stated that if he was rich, he wouldn't
       have had to loan the money.

75. From the point of view of current correct English usage     75.\_\_\_
    and grammar, the MOST acceptable of the following
    sentences is:
    A. Before beginning the investigation, all the materials
       relating to the case were carefully assembled.
    B. The reason for his inability to keep the appointment
       is because of his injury in the accident.
    C. This here evidence tends to support the claim of the
       defendant.
    D. We interviewed all the witnesses who, according to
       the driver, were still in town.

# KEY (CORRECT ANSWERS)

| | | |
|---|---|---|
| 1. C | 26. B | 51. B |
| 2. C | 27. D | 52. B |
| 3. A | 28. A | 53. A |
| 4. D | 29. B | 54. B |
| 5. B | 30. C | 55. D |
| 6. B | 31. D | 56. A |
| 7. D | 32. B | 57. D |
| 8. D | 33. D | 58. C |
| 9. A | 34. B | 59. A |
| 10. A | 35. B | 60. B |
| 11. A | 36. A | 61. D |
| 12. D | 37. B | 62. C |
| 13. D | 38. A | 63. C |
| 14. C | 39. B | 64. A |
| 15. A | 40. C | 65. C |
| 16. B | 41. D | 66. C |
| 17. D | 42. A | 67. B |
| 18. D | 43. D | 68. D |
| 19. B | 44. A | 69. B |
| 20. C | 45. D | 70. D |
| 21. A | 46. C | 71. D |
| 22. C | 47. B | 72. B |
| 23. B | 48. A | 73. A |
| 24. C | 49. C | 74. C |
| 25. C | 50. A | 75. D |

# EXAMINATION SECTION

DIRECTIONS: Each question or incomplete statement is followed by several suggested answers or completions. Select the one that BEST answers the question or completes the statement. *PRINT THE LETTER OF THE CORRECT ANSWER IN THE SPACE AT THE RIGHT.*

1. The BEST reason, among the following, for obtaining a   1.___
written and signed statement of the testimony of a witness
is that
   A. unless reduced to writing, it cannot ultimately be
      placed in evidence in court
   B. the witness may be unavailable at the time of a sub-
      sequent trial or may attempt to change his testimony
   C. the investigator's notes of the interview may be
      defective or incomplete
   D. such a written statement becomes *best evidence*
      whereas the investigator's report is mere hearsay

2. When an investigator hears an important statement made by   2.___
a witness and the witness is not willing to reduce the
statement to writing, the MOST advisable of the following
procedures for the investigator to follow is to
   A. write it himself and have the witness sign it if he
      is willing to do so
   B. write it himself and insist that the witness sign it
   C. write it himself, making sure the witness does not
      see it
   D. threaten to write it himself if the witness will not
      do so

3. Suppose that you are interviewing an eleven-year-old boy.   3.___
The CHIEF point, among the following, for you to keep in
mind is that a child, as compared with an adult, is
generally
   A. more likely to attempt to conceal information
   B. a person of lower intelligence
   C. more garrulous
   D. more receptive to suggestive questions

4. Of the following, witnesses to the same event should be   4.___
interviewed
   A. *together* so that each can help to refresh the recol-
      lection of the others
   B. *together* so that discrepancies in their statements
      can be corrected more readily
   C. *separately* since many persons refuse to speak in the
      presence of others
   D. *separately* to prevent the testimony of one from
      coloring the testimony of the others

5. When a witness is reluctant to talk because he does not          5.___
   like to be involved in litigation, the MOST advisable
   of the following procedures for the investigator is to
      A. be as gentle as possible and interrogate in the form
         of casual questions and conversation
      B. attempt to give the witness a new interest or motive
         for testifying
      C. use a device, such as the association method, to
         elicit the desired information
      D. proceed with sternness and determination, warning
         the witness of the serious consequences of his
         refusal

6. If a person you are interviewing in connection with a          6.___
   character investigation obviously is not telling the
   truth, the MOST advisable of the following procedures
   is to
      A. let him talk as much as he likes so that he may
         eventually contradict himself and tell the truth
      B. threaten him with criminal prosecution if he does
         not tell the truth
      C. administer an oath to him before he is questioned
      D. disregard his testimony entirely and question him
         no further

7. In the course of a routine investigation of sales tax          7.___
   payments, the examination of a firm's books discloses
   to the investigator evidence that the firm's bookkeeper
   may be appropriating large sums of the firm's funds to
   his own use.
   The investigator's BEST course of action, among the
   following, would be to
      A. warn the bookkeeper of his discovery but take no
         further action since his obligations are toward
         the city not the firm
      B. advise the firm of his suspicions, suggesting an
         audit of the books
      C. immediately report his findings to the District
         Attorney
      D. take no action other than to include the evidence
         among the findings in his report

8. Information obtained by an investigator from a very          8.___
   small child should be carefully evaluated because, of
   the following reasons, children
      A. are less observing than adults
      B. have less retentive memories
      C. easily confuse their own experiences with those of
         others
      D. are apt to have been coached by adults

9. In the course of an investigation of a claim for damages     9.___
   for personal injuries sustained by an individual, an
   anonymous letter is received by the investigator accusing
   this individual of mistreating his wife and children.
   The MOST advisable of the following courses of action
   for the investigator to pursue is
   - A. as a law enforcement officer,to report the matter to
     the proper authorities
   - B. to place less credence in the testimony given by the
     individual in view of this impeachment of his
     character
   - C. to attempt to trace the letter and inquire further
     into the allegations made therein before submitting
     his report
   - D. to disregard the letter since it has no direct bearing
     on the matter under investigation

10. In interviewing a person, *suggestive questions* should be     10.___
    avoided because, among the following,
    - A. the answers to leading questions are not admissible
      in evidence
    - B. an investigator must be fair and impartial
    - C. the interrogation of a witness must be formulated
      according to his mentality
    - D. they are less apt to lead to the truth

11. Among the following, it is GENERALLY desirable to inter-     11.___
    view a person outside his home or office because
    - A. the presence of relatives and friends may prevent
      him from speaking freely
    - B. a person's surroundings tend to color his testimony
    - C. the person will find less distraction outside his
      home or office
    - D. a person tends to dominate the interview when in
      familiar surroundings

12. Even when an investigator is convinced of the honesty     12.___
    and truthfulness of a witness, thorough checking of all
    reported information with physical facts is imperative
    because, among the following,
    - A. mere parole testimony is not accepted as legal
      evidence
    - B. the observation of the witness may have been imper-
      fect due to some factors which distort normal
      sensory perception
    - C. the physical facts may have changed since they were
      observed by the witness
    - D. an interview with a witness is merely an informal
      questioning conducted to learn facts

13. If the memory of a witness fails him about the time of an   13.___
occurrence concerning which he is being questioned, the
MOST advisable of the following procedures for the inves-
tigator to follow is to
   A. supply the data for him in his report
   B. assume the presence of a motive for concealing the
      information
   C. request him to make an affidavit to that effect
   D. try to give him some associated ideas to refresh
      his memory

14. If a person interviewed seems hesitant to talk while the   14.___
investigator is taking notes, the MOST advisable of the
following procedures for the investigator is to
   A. adjourn the interview until a time when it can be
      conducted in a place with a hidden microphone to
      record it
   B. secure his cooperation by explaining to the witness
      the importance of full and complete notes for good
      investigation reports
   C. complete the interview without notetaking and, at
      the first opportunity after the interview, reduce it
      to writing
   D. administer an oath to the person so that he will
      commit perjury by failing to tell the whole truth

15. The personal interview as a means of obtaining informa-   15.___
tion about past occurrences is
   A. the most reliable and accurate method
   B. useful principally as a means of finding clues to
      more reliable sources of information
   C. generally as reliable as recourse to documentary
      sources
   D. qualitatively inferior but quantitatively superior
      to all other methods

16. Experiments have shown that the MOST satisfactory method,   16.___
among the following, for obtaining dependable data in an
interview is by employment of
   A. the free narrative method, in which the person
      interviewed is permitted to talk without interrup-
      tion
   B. the question-and-answer method, in which the person
      interviewed gives information only in response to
      questions
   C. a combination of the question-and-answer and free
      narrative methods, with the free narrative given
      first
   D. a combination of the question-and-answer and free
      narrative methods, with the question-and-answer
      interview given first

17. Interviewing witnesses by the question-and-answer method,    17.\_\_\_
rather than allowing the witness to tell his story with-
out interruption, will GENERALLY \_\_\_\_\_ accuracy of the
report.
   A. *increase* the range but decrease the
   B. *decrease* the range but increase the
   C. *decrease* both the range and
   D. *increase* both the range and

18. Among the following, the present good health of a    18.\_\_\_
disabled war veteran is BEST indicated by
   A. a recently issued life insurance policy
   B. a return to his pre-war employment as a cashier
   C. his withdrawal of a civil service veteran preference
   claim
   D. a reduction in the amount of his pension by the
   Veterans Administration

19. Among the following, a person's general good character    19.\_\_\_
is BEST evidenced by
   A. the absence of an F.B.I. record
   B. a Police Department good conduct certificate
   C. his school and employment records
   D. letters of recommendation he obtains from friends

20. Among the following, the signature cards of a bank might    20.\_\_\_
be employed as a means of verifying an individual's
   A. character          B. identity
   C. financial status   D. employment

21. Of the following, the overt item of evidence which most    21.\_\_\_
strongly indicates that an adult person is probably NOT
a citizen is
   A. the fact he associates frequently with recently
   arrived aliens
   B. his lack of a birth certificate
   C. his inability to speak English
   D. the fact his parents are aliens

22. Among the following, an original birth certificate may    22.\_\_\_
serve as proof of age and
   A. physical condition    B. religion
   C. citizenship           D. residence

23. *Prima facie* evidence is evidence which    23.\_\_\_
   A. suffices to establish a fact unless rebutted or
   until overcome by other evidence
   B. has not been tested or measured as to its validity
   C. shows the existence of one fact by proof of the
   existence of other facts from which the first may
   be inferred
   D. results from certain presumptions of law, which
   may not have a basis in fact

6

24. A copy, accompanied by a certificate of the proceedings necessary to be taken in order to authorize the same to be entered of record, is called a(n) _____ copy.
   A. exemplified          B. certified
   C. true                 D. verified

24.___

25. The term *surveillance*, as used in connection with investigations, is synonymous with
   A. undercover work      B. reconnaissance
   C. shadowing            D. inspection

25.___

26. An investigation manual directs that all investigators' reports contain a precis.
The term *precis* is synonymous with
   A. extract              B. paraphrase
   C. synopsis             D. conclusion

26.___

27. A sworn statement made by the person who served a summons, setting forth the place and manner of service, is called a(n) _____ of service.
   A. admission            B. affidavit
   C. certificate          D. acknowledgment

27.___

28. A book in which deeds are recorded in the City Registrar's Office is referred to as a
   A. text      B. folio      C. volume      D. liber

28.___

29. The system of describing persons that is GENERALLY employed by modern investigators is known as the _____ system.
   A. Bertillion           B. Henry
   C. Moulage              D. Portrait Parle

29.___

30. A satisfaction piece is an instrument
   A. which purports to discharge land from the lien of a mortgage
   B. by which pending litigation is settled out of court
   C. acknowledging payment of a money judgment
   D. by which a lien on personal property is discharged

30.___

31. The part of an instrument which reads: *Sworn to before me this eighteenth day of July, 1990, Joseph Smith, Notary Public, State of* ..... is known as the
   A. jurat                B. authentication
   C. certification        D. attestation

31.___

32. An authority for the arrest of a person on a criminal charge with a view to his trial and commitment thereon is called a
   A. subpoena    B. summons    C. complaint    D. warrant

32.___

33. Entries on the block index sheets for conveyances in the     33.___
    city Registrar's Office are made in _____ order.
    A. alphabetical            B. date
    C. numerical               D. no particular

34. Generally, a summons may be served                           34.___
    A. at any hour of the day or night any day of the week
    B. between sunrise and sunset on any day of the week
    C. at any hour of the day or night, any day of the week,
       except Sunday
    D. between sunrise and sunset on any day of the week,
       except Sunday

35. A party refuses to accept service of a summons when          35.___
    properly offered him.
    Among the following methods, personal service upon him
    could be properly made after informing him of the nature
    of the instrument by
    A. thrusting the summons into his lap or upon his person
    B. sending the summons to him by registered mail
    C. leaving the summons on a table before him in his
       presence
    D. leaving the summons with another member of his
       household

36. In an action against the city, personal service of the       36.___
    summons is made by delivering a copy thereof to the
    mayor,
    A. treasurer, or city clerk
    B. comptroller or city clerk
    C. treasurer or corporation counsel
    D. comptroller or corporation counsel

37. Among the following, the present home and business           37.___
    address of a member of the board of directors of a city
    bank may MOST readily be obtained from
    A. MOODY'S BANK AND FINANCE DIRECTORY
    B. POOR'S REGISTER
    C. TROW'S CITY DIRECTORY
    D. DAU'S BLUE BOOK

38. Among the following, a list of the names and addresses       38.___
    of various professional associations and societies in
    the United States would be found in the
    A. WORLD ALMANAC          B. ENCYCLOPEDIA BRITANNICA
    C. CONGRESSIONAL RECORD    D. POOR'S REGISTER

39. Workmen's Compensation claims are filed with the             39.___
    A. Comptroller
    B. State Department of Labor
    C. United States Department of Labor
    D. Municipal Compensation Board

40. The Bureau of Narcotics is part of the United States                    40.___
    A. Department of Agriculture
    B. Department of Commerce
    C. Treasury Department
    D. Justice Department

Questions 41-49.

DIRECTIONS:  Questions 41 through 49 are to be answered on the
             basis of the following passage.

*Assume that in an interview John Jones, the subject of an
investigation, gave the following information concerning himself:*

*I was born on January 5, 1948 in a hospital in Manhattan.  My
parents resided in Brooklyn at the time.  My mother was born in
this country, but my father was born in England and came to this
country with his parents when he was about eighteen years old.  I
attended P.S. 300 in Brooklyn from 1954 to 1962 and Central High
School in Brooklyn from 1962 to 1966.  From 1966 to 1972, I was
employed as a clerk by the XYZ Corporation, which has since gone out
of business and been dissolved.  In 1972, I was inducted into the
Army at Fort Dix, New Jersey, from Selective Service Board No. 528,
Brooklyn.  I served with the 1097th Infantry Regiment until my
discharge on December 1, 1975.  Since then, I have been employed as
a merchant seaman on the U.S. Barclay by the Red Circle Steamship
Company.*

41. Among the following, Jones' birth record should be sought    41.___
    in the
    A. County Clerk's Office of the county in which he was
       born
    B. City Clerk's Office
    C. Department of Health
    D. Register's Office

42. If no record of Jones' birth is available there and he       42.___
    has no baptismal record, among the following, his date
    of birth may BEST be verified from the records of
    A. P.S. 300, Brooklyn
    B. the Board of Elections
    C. Draft Board No. 528, Brooklyn
    D. the XYZ Corporation

43. Among the following, Jones' father's citizenship can be      43.___
    verified through records of the
    A. Department of State
    B. Immigration and Naturalization Service
    C. Federal Bureau of Investigation
    D. U.S. Customs Service

44. If, in verifying Jones' education, it is desirable to        44.\_\_\_
    write to the principal of Central High School, among
    the following, his full name and the address of the
    school will be found in the
    A. Brooklyn Telephone Directory
    B. NEW YORK CITY OFFICIAL DIRECTORY (THE GREEN BOOK)
    C. Civil List
    D. DIRECTORY OF AMERICAN SCHOOLS AND COLLEGES

45. Among the following, data regarding the now defunct         45.\_\_\_
    XYZ Corporation could BEST be obtained from the records
    of the
    A. New York City Department of Commerce
    B. United States Department of Commerce
    C. Secretary of State of New York State
    D. Attorney General of New York State

46. Among the following, an inquiry regarding Jones' military  46.\_\_\_
    service should be addressed to the
    A. Chairman, Selective Service Board No. 528, Brooklyn,
       N.Y.
    B. Adjutant General, The Pentagon, Washington, D.C.
    C. Commanding Officer, 1097th Infantry Regiment, Defense
       Department, Washington, D.C.
    D. Regional Office, Veterans Administration, Brooklyn,
       N.Y.

47. Among the following, if none of the officers of the XYZ    47.\_\_\_
    Corporation can be located, Jones' employment with that
    Corporation might BEST be verified from the records of
    the
    A. State Department of Labor
    B. Secretary of State
    C. Social Security Administration
    D. Superintendent of Insurance

48. Among the following, data regarding Jones' financial       48.\_\_\_
    and credit status can BEST be obtained from
    A. R.L. POLK DIRECTORY      B. DUN AND BRADSTREET'S
    C. Municipal Credit Union   D. Tax Department

49. If Jones did not want his present employer to know of      49.\_\_\_
    the pending investigation, from among the following,
    his employment on the S.S. Barclay could be verified
    from the records of the
    A. U.S. Maritime Commission
    B. Bureau of Customs
    C. Port of New York Authority
    D. Department of Marine and Aviation

Questions 50-57.

DIRECTIONS: Column I lists various records or instruments. Column II lists various public offices. In the space at the right, opposite the number preceding each of the records or instruments in Column I, place the letter preceding the public office in Column II in which such record or information concerning such instrument may be obtained.

COLUMN I

COLUMN II

50. Voting records

51. Record of deaths

52. Record of marriages performed in 1985

53. Record of marriages performed in 1905

54. Birth certificates

55. Lis pendens in a real property action

56. Will relating to real property

57. Certificate of appointment of a notary public

A. County Clerk's Office        50.___

B. Surrogate's Office           51.___

C. Board of Elections           52.___

D. Department of Health
                                53.___

                                54.___

                                55.___

                                56.___

                                57.___

Questions 58-66.

DIRECTIONS: Column I lists various records. Column II lists various governmental departments and offices. In the space at the right, opposite the number preceding each of the records in Column I, place the letter preceding the department or office in Column II from which you would seek information regarding such record.

COLUMN I

COLUMN II

58. Real estate tax assessment rolls

59. Compensating use tax records

60. Personal injury claims against the city

61. Licenses as Commissioner of Deeds

A. Health Department            58.___

B. Comptroller's Office
                                59.___
C. City Register's Office

D. Department of Finance        60.___

E. Department of Licenses
                                61.___
F. Police Department

| COLUMN I | COLUMN II | |
|---|---|---|
| 62. Pawnbroker's license records | G. City Marshal | 62.___ |
| 63. Pistol license records | H. Tax Department | 63.___ |
| 64. Zoning regulations | I. Bureau of Real Estate | 64.___ |
| 65. Real estate mortgage records | J. City Clerk's Office | 65.___ |
| 66. Public assistance records | K. City Planning Commission | |
| | L. Welfare Department | 66.___ |

Questions 67-74.

DIRECTIONS: Column I lists various licenses and records. Column II lists various state departments and offices. In the space at the right, opposite the number preceding each of the licenses or records in Column I, place the letter preceding the department or office in Column II from which you would seek information regarding such license or record.

| COLUMN I | COLUMN II | |
|---|---|---|
| 67. Bailbondsman's license | A. Secretary of State | 67.___ |
| 68. Retail liquor store permit | B. Department of Education | 68.___ |
| 69. Certificate of incorporation of stock corporation | C. Department of Taxation and Finance | 69.___ |
| 70. Real estate broker's license | D. Department of Audit and Control | 70.___ |
| 71. Physician's license | | 71.___ |
| 72. Income tax records | E. Alcoholic Beverage Control Division | 72.___ |
| 73. License as private investigator | F. Division of Parole | 73.___ |
| 74. State criminal identification records | G. Department of Correction | |
| | H. Department of Labor | |
| | I. Banking Department | |
| | J. Insurance Department | |
| | K. Department of Social Services | |

Questions 75-80.

DIRECTIONS:  Column I lists various records or instruments. Column II
             lists various federal departments or offices. In the
             space at the right, opposite the number preceding each
             of the records or instruments in Column I, place the
             letter preceding the office or department in Column II
             from which information regarding such record or instru-
             ment may be obtained.

| COLUMN I | COLUMN II | |
|---|---|---|
| 75. Passport records | A. Department of State | 75.___ |
| 76. Register of copyrights | B. Library of Congress | 76.___ |
| 77. Federal income tax records | C. U.S. District Court | 77.___ |
| 78. World War II draft records | D. Social Security Administration | 78.___ |
| 79. Immigration visas | | 79.___ |
| 80. Bankruptcy petitions | E. U.S. Patent Office | 80.___ |
| | F. Office of Selective Service Records | |
| | G. Internal Revenue Bureau | |
| | H. Adjutant General's Office | |
| | I. Department of Justice | |

# KEY (CORRECT ANSWERS)

| | | | |
|---|---|---|---|
| 1. B | 21. C | 41. C | 61. J |
| 2. A | 22. C | 42. A | 62. E |
| 3. D | 23. A | 43. B | 63. F |
| 4. D | 24. A | 44. B | 64. K |
| 5. B | 25. C | 45. C | 65. C |
| | | | |
| 6. A | 26. C | 46. B | 66. L |
| 7. B | 27. B | 47. C | 67. J |
| 8. C | 28. D | 48. B | 68. E |
| 9. D | 29. D | 49. A | 69. A |
| 10. D | 30. A | 50. C | 70. A |
| | | | |
| 11. A | 31. A | 51. D | 71. B |
| 12. B | 32. D | 52. A | 72. C |
| 13. D | 33. B | 53. D | 73. A |
| 14. C | 34. C | 54. D | 74. G |
| 15. B | 35. C | 55. A | 75. A |
| | | | |
| 16. C | 36. D | 56. B | 76. B |
| 17. A | 37. B | 57. A | 77. G |
| 18. A | 38. A | 58. H | 78. F |
| 19. C | 39. B | 59. B | 79. A |
| 20. B | 40. D | 60. B | 80. C |

# EXAMINATION SECTION

## TEST 1

DIRECTIONS: Each question or incomplete statement is followed by several suggested answers or completions. Select the one that BEST answers the question or completes the statement. *PRINT THE LETTER OF THE CORRECT ANSWER IN THE SPACE AT THE RIGHT.*

1. An investigator uses *Forms A, B,* and *C* in filling out his investigation reports. He uses *Form B* five times as often as *Form A,* and he uses *Form C* three times as often as *Form B.*
   If the total number of all forms used by the investigator in a month equals 735, HOW MANY TIMES was *Form B* used?
      A. 150     B. 175     C. 205     D. 235     1.___

2. Of all the investigators in one agency, 25% work in a particular building. Of these, 12% have desks on the 14th floor.
   What PERCENTAGE of the investigators work in this building but do NOT have desks on the 14th floor?
      A. 12%     B. 13%     C. 22%     D. 23%     2.___

3. An investigator is given two reports to read. *Report P* is 160 pages long and takes the investigator 3 hours and 20 minutes to read.
   If *Report S* is 254 pages long and the investigator reads it at the same rate as he reads *Report P,* HOW LONG will it take him to read *Report S?* ____ hours ____ minutes.
      A. 4; 15     B. 4; 50     C. 5; 10     D. 5; 30     3.___

4. A team of 6 investigators was assigned to interview 234 people.
   If half the investigators conduct twice as many interviews as the other half, and the slow group interviews 12 persons a day, HOW MANY DAYS would it take to complete this assignment? ____ days.
      A. $4\frac{1}{4}$     B. 5     C. 6     D. $6\frac{1}{2}$     4.___

5. The investigators in one agency conduct an average of 12 interviews an hour from 10 A.M. to 12 noon and from 1 P.M. to 5 P.M. daily. The director of this agency knows from past experience that 20% of those called in to be interviewed are unable to keep the appointments that were scheduled.
   If the director wants his staff to be kept occupied with interviews for the entire time period that has been set aside for this function, HOW MANY appointments should be scheduled for each day?
      A. 86     B. 90     C. 96     D. 101     5.___

6. An investigator has a 430 page report to read. The first      6.___
   day, he is able to read 20 pages. The second day, he reads
   10 pages more than the first day, and the third day, he
   reads 15 pages more than the second day.
   If, on the following days, he continues to read at the same
   rate he was reading on the third day, he will COMPLETE the
   report on the ____ day.
   A. 7th              B. 8th              C. 10th            D. 11th

7. The 36 investigators in an agency are each required to       7.___
   submit 25 investigation reports a week. These reports are
   filled out on a certain form, and only one copy of the
   form is needed per report.
   Allowing 20% for waste , HOW MANY packages of 45 forms a
   piece should be ordered for each weekly period?
   A. 15              B. 20              C. 25              D. 30

8. During the fiscal year, an investigative unit received      8.___
   $260 for stationery and telephone expenditures. It spent
   43% for stationery and 1/3 of the balance for telephone
   service.
   The amount of money that was left at the end of the fiscal
   year was MOST NEARLY
   A. $49             B. $50             C. $99             D. $109

Questions 9-10.

DIRECTIONS: Answer Questions 9 and 10 SOLELY on the data given below.

| Number of days absent per worker (sickness) | 1 | 2 | 3 | 4 | 5 | 6 | 7 | 8 or Over |
|---|---|---|---|---|---|---|---|---|
| Number of workers | 96 | 45 | 16 | 3 | 1 | 0 | 1 | 0 |

Total Number of Workers: 500
Period Covered: Jan. 1, 1986 - Dec. 31, 1986

9. The TOTAL number of man days lost due to illness in 1986     9.___
   was
   A. 137             B. 154             C. 162             D. 258

10. Of the 500 workers studied, the number who lost NO days     10.___
    due to sickness in 1986 was
    A. 230             B. 298             C. 338             D. 372

Questions 11-13.

DIRECTIONS: Answer Questions 11 to 13 SOLELY on the basis of the
            following paragraphs.

*The rise of urban-industrial society has complicated the social
arrangements needed to regulate contacts between people. As a conse-
quence, there has been an unprecedented increase in the volume of laws
and regulations designed to control individual conduct and to govern
the relationship of the individual to others. In a century, there has
been an eight-fold increase in the crimes for which one may be prosecute*

*For these offences, the courts have the ultimate responsibility for redressing wrongs and convicting the guilty. The body of legal precepts gives the impression of an abstract and evenhanded dispensation of justice. Actually, the personnel of the agencies applying these precepts are faced with the difficulties of fitting abstract principles to highly variable situations emerging from the dynamics of everyday life. It is inevitable that discrepancies should exist between precept and practice.*

*The legal institutions serve as a framework for the social order by their slowness to respond to the caprices of transitory fad. This valuable contribution exacts a price in terms of the inflexibility of legal institutions in responding to new circumstances. This possibility is promoted by the changes in values and norms of the dynamic larger culture of which the legal precepts are a part.*

11. According to the above passage, the increase in the number of laws and regulations during the twentieth century can be attributed to the    11.___
    A. complexity of modern industrial society
    B. increased seriousness of offenses committed
    C. growth of individualism
    D. anonymity of urban living

12. According to the above passage, which of the following presents a problem to the staff of legal agencies? The    12.___
    A. need to eliminate the discrepancy between precept and practice
    B. necessity to apply abstract legal precepts to rapidly changing conditions
    C. responsibility for reducing the number of abstract legal principles
    D. responsibility for understanding offenses in terms of the real-life situations from which they emerge

13. According to the above passage, it can be concluded that legal institutions affect social institutions by    13.___
    A. preventing change
    B. keeping pace with its norms and values
    C. changing its norms and values
    D. providing stability

Questions 14-16.

DIRECTIONS:  Answer Questions 14 through 16 SOLELY on the basis of information given in the passage below.

*A personnel interviewer, selecting job applicants, may find that he reacts badly to some people even on first contact. This reaction cannot usually be explained by things that the interviewee has done or said. Most of us have had the experience of liking or disliking, of feeling comfortable or uncomfortable with people on first acquaintance, long before we have had a chance to make a conscious, rational decision about them. Often, too, our liking or disliking is transmitted to the other person by subtle processes such as gestures, posture, voice intonations, or choice of words. The point to be kept in mind is this:*

*the relations between people are complex and occur at several levels, from the conscious to the unconscious. This is true whether the relationship is brief or long, formal or informal.*

*Some of the major dynamics of personality which operate on the unconscious level are projection, sublimation, rationalization, and repression. Encountering these for the first time, one is apt to think of them as representing pathological states. In the extreme, they undoubtedly are, but they exist so universally that we must consider them also to be parts of normal personality.*

*Without necessarily subscribing to any of the numerous theories of personality, it is possible to describe personality in terms of certain important aspects or elements. We are all aware of ourselves as thinking organisms.*

*This aspect of personality, the conscious part, is important for understanding human behavior, but it is not enough. Many find it hard to accept the notion that each person also has an unconscious. The existence of the unconscious is no longer a matter of debate. It is not possible to estimate at all precisely what proportion of our total psychological life is conscious, what proportion unconscious. Everyone who has studied the problem, however, agrees that consciousness is the smaller part of personality. Most of what we are and do is a result of unconscious processes. To ignore this is to risk mistakes.*

14. The passage above suggests that an interviewer can be MOST effective if he    14.___
    A. learns how to determine other peoples' unconscious motivations
    B. learns how to repress his own unconsciously motivated mannerisms and behavior
    C. can keep others from feeling that he either likes or dislikes them
    D. gains an understanding of how the unconscious operates in himself and in others

15. It may be inferred from the passage above that the *subtle processes such as gestures, posture, voice intonation, or choice of words* referred to in the first paragraph are USUALLY    15.___
    A. in the complete control of an expert investigator
    B. the determining factors in the friendships a person establishes
    C. controlled by a person's unconscious
    D. not capable of being consciously controlled

16. The passage above implies that various different personality theories are USUALLY    16.___
    A. so numerous and different as to be valueless to an investigator
    B. in basic agreement about the importance of the unconscious
    C. understood by the investigator who strives to be effective
    D. in agreement that personality factors such as projection and repression are pathological

Questions 17-19

DIRECTIONS: Questions 17 through 19 are to be answered SOLELY on the basis of information contained in the following passage.

*No matter how well the interrogator adjusts himself to the witness and how precisely he induces the witness to describe his observations, mistakes still can be made. The mistakes made by an experienced interrogator may be comparatively few, but as far as the witness is concerned, his path is full of pitfalls. Modern "witness psychology" has shown that even the most honest and trustworthy witnesses are apt to make grave mistakes in good faith. It is, therefore, necessary that the interrogator get an idea of the weak links in the testimony in order to check up on them in the event that something appears to be strange or not quite satisfactory.*

*Unfortunately, modern witness psychology does not yet offer any means of directly testing the credibility of testimony. It lacks precision and method, in spite of worthwhile attempts on the part of learned men. At the same time, witness psychology, through the gathering of many experiences concerning the weaknesses of human testimony, has been of invaluable service. It shows clearly that only evidence of a technical nature has absolute value as proof.*

*Testimony may be separated into the following stages: (1) perception; (2) observation; (3) mind fixation of the observed occurrences, in which fantasy, association of ideas, and personal judgment participate; (4) expression in oral or written form, where the testimony is transferred from one witness to another or to the interrogator.*

*Each of these stages offers innumerable possibilities for the distortion of testimony.*

17. The passage above indicates that having witnesses talk to each other before testifying is a practice which is GENERALLY    17.___
    A. *desirable*, since the witnesses will be able to correct each other's errors in observation before testimony
    B. *undesirable*, since the witnesses will collaborate on one story to tell the investigator
    C. *undesirable*, since one witness may distort his testimony because of what another witness may erroneously say
    D. *desirable*, since witnesses will become aware of discrepancies in their own testimony and can point out the discrepancies to the investigator

18. According to the above passage, the one of the following which would be the MOST reliable for use as evidence would be the testimony of a    18.___
    A. handwriting expert about a signature on a forged check
    B. trained police officer about the identity of a criminal
    C. laboratory technician about an accident he has observed
    D. psychologist who has interviewed any witnesses who relate conflicting stories

19. Concerning the validity of evidence, it is CLEAR from the        19.___
    above passage that
        A. only evidence of a technical nature is at all valuable
        B. the testimony of witnesses is so flawed that it is
           usually valueless
        C. an investigator, by knowing modern witness psychology,
           will usually be able to perceive mistaken testimony
        D. an investigator ought to expect mistakes in even the
           most reliable witness testimony

Questions 20-21.

DIRECTIONS:  Answer Questions 20 and 21 SOLELY on the basis of
             information given in the passage below.

*Since we generally assure informants that what they say is con-
fidential, we are not free to tell one informant what the other has
told us. Even if the informant says, "I don't care who knows it;
tell anybody you want to," we find it wise to treat the interview as
confidential. An interviewer who relates to some informants what
other informants have told him is likely to stir up anxiety and suspicion. Of course, the interviewer may be able to tell an informant
what he has heard without revealing the source of his information.
This may be perfectly appropriate where a story has wide currency so
that an informant cannot infer the source of the information. But
if an event is not widely known, the mere mention of it may reveal
to one informant what another informant has said about the situation.
How can the data be cross-checked in these circumstances?*

20. The passage above IMPLIES that the anxiety and suspicion      20.___
    an interviewer may arouse by telling what has been learned
    in other interviews is due to the
        A. lack of trust the person interviewed may have in the
           interviewer's honesty
        B. troublesome nature of the material which the inter-
           viewer has learned in other interviews
        C. fact that the person interviewed may not believe that
           permission was given to repeat the information
        D. fear of the person interviewed that what he is telling
           the interviewer will be repeated

21. The paragraph above is MOST likely part of a longer passage 21.___
    dealing with
        A. ways to verify data gathered in interviews
        B. the various anxieties a person being interviewed may
           feel
        C. the notion that people sometimes say things they do
           not mean
        D. ways an interviewer can avoid seeming suspicious

Questions 22-23.

DIRECTIONS:  Answer Questions 22 and 23 SOLELY on the basis of
             information given below.

*The ability to interview rests not on any single trait, but on a vast complex of them. Habits, skills, techniques, and attitudes are all involved. Competence in interviewing is acquired only after careful and diligent study, prolonged practice (preferably under super- vision), and a good bit of trial and error; for interviewing is not an exact science, it is an art. Like many other arts, however, it can and must draw on science in several of its aspects.*

*There is always a place for individual initiative, for imagina- tive innovations, and for new combinations of old approaches. The skilled interviewer cannot be bound by a set of rules. Likewise, there is not a set of rules which can guarantee to the novice that his inter- viewing will be successful. There are, however, some accepted, general guideposts which may help the beginner to avoid mistakes, learn how to conserve his efforts, and establish effective working relationships with interviewees; to accomplish, in short, what he sets out to do.*

22. According to the passage above, rules and standard     22.___
    techniques for interviewing are
    A. helpful for the beginner, but useless for the experi- enced, innovative interviewer
    B. destructive of the innovation and initiative needed for a good interviewer
    C. useful for even the experienced interviewer, who may, however, sometimes go beyond them
    D. the means by which nearly anybody can become an effective interviewer

23. According to the passage above, the one of the following     23.___
    which is a PREREQUISITE to competent interviewing is
    A. avoid mistakes          B. study and practice
    C. imaginative innovation  D. natural aptitude

Questions 24-27.

DIRECTIONS:  Answer Questions 24 through 27 SOLELY on the basis of information given in the following paragraph.

*The question of what material is relevant is not as simple as it might seem. Frequently, material which seems irrelevant to the inex- perienced has, because of the common tendency to disguise and distort and misplace one's feelings, considerable significance. It may be necessary to let the client "ramble on" for a while in order to clear the decks, as it were, so that he may get down to things that really are on his mind. On the other hand, with an already disturbed person, it may be important for the interviewer to know when to discourage further elaboration of upsetting material. This is especially the case where the worker would be unable to do anything about it. An in- experienced interviewer might, for instance, be intrigued with the bizarre elaboration of material that the psychotic produces, but fur- ther elaboration of this might encourage the client in his instability. A too random discussion may indicate that the interviewee is not certain in what areas the interviewer is prepared to help him, and he may be seeking some direction. Or again, satisfying though it may be for the interviewer to have the interviewee tell him intimate details, such revelations sometimes need to be checked or encouraged only in small doses. An interviewee who has "talked too much" often reveals subsequent anxiety. This is illustrated by the fact that frequently after a "confessional" interview, the interviewee surprises the interviewer by being withdrawn, inarticulate, or hostile, or by breaking the next appointment.*

24. Sometimes a client may reveal certain personal information  24.___
to an interviewer and subsequently may feel anxious about
this revelation.
If, during an interview, a client begins to discuss very
personal matters, it would be BEST to
   A. tell the client, in no uncertain terms, that you're
   not interested in personal details
   B. ignore the client at this point
   C. encourage the client to elaborate further on the details
   D. inform the client that the information seems to be
   very personal

25. The author indicates that clients with severe psychologi-  25.___
cal disturbances pose an especially difficult problem for
the inexperienced interviewer.
The DIFFICULTY lies in the possibility of the client
   A. becoming physically violent and harming the interviewer
   B. *rambling on* for a while
   C. revealing irrelevant details which may be followed by
   cancelled appointments
   D. reverting to an unstable state as a result of inter-
   view material

26. An interviewer should be constantly alert to the possibil-  26.___
ity of obtaining clues from the client as to the problem
areas.
According to the above passage, a client who discusses
topics at random may be
   A. unsure of what problems the interviewer can provide
   help with
   B. reluctant to discuss intimate details
   C. trying to impress the interviewer with his knowledge
   D. deciding what relevant material to elaborate on

27. The evaluation of a client's responses may reveal substan-  27.___
tial information that may aid the interviewer in assessing
the problem areas that are of concern to the client.
Responses that seemed irrelevant at the time of the interview may be of significance because
   A. considerable significance is attached to all irrelevant
   material
   B. emotional feelings are frequently masked
   C. an initial *rambling on* is often a prelude to what is
   actually bothering the client
   D. disturbed clients often reveal subsequent anxiety

Questions 28-30.

DIRECTIONS:    Answer Questions 28 through 30 SOLELY on the basis of
               the following paragraph.

*The physical setting of the interview may determine its entire
potentiality. Some degree of privacy and a comfortable relaxed atmosphere are important. The interviewee is not encouraged to give
much more than his name and address if the interviewer seems busy
with other things, if people are rushing about, if there are distrac-
ting noises. He has a right to feel that, whether the interview lasts
five minutes or an hour, he has, for that time, the undivided attention
of the interviewer. Interruptions, telephone calls, and so on, should
be reduced to a minimum. If the interviewee has waited in a crowded
room for what seems to him an interminably long period, he is naturally
in no mood to sit down and discuss what is on his mind. Indeed, by
that time, the primary thing on his mind may be his irritation at being
kept waiting, and he frequently feels it would be impolite to express
this. If a wait or interruptions have been unavoidable, it is always
helpful to give the client some recognition that these are disturbing
and that we can naturally understand that they make it more difficult
for him to proceed. At the same time, if he protests that they have
not troubled him, the interviewer can best accept his statements at
their face value, as further insistence that they must have been disturbing may be interpreted by him as accusing, and he may conclude
that the interviewer has been personally hurt by his irritation.*

28.  Distraction during an interview may tend to limit the              28.____
     client's responses.
     In a case where an interruption has occurred, it would be
     BEST for the investigator to
         A. terminate this interview and have it rescheduled for
            another time period
         B. ignore the interruption since it is not continuous
         C. express his understanding that the distraction can
            cause the client to feel disturbed
         D. accept the client's protests that he has been troubled
            by the interruption

29.  To maximize the rapport that can be established with the           29.____
     client, an appropriate physical setting is necessary.  At
     the very least, some privacy would be necessary.
     In ADDITION, the interviewer should
         A. always appear to be busy in order to impress the client
         B. focus his attention only on the client
         C. accept all the client's statements as being valid
         D. stress the importance of the interview to the client

30.  Clients who have been waiting quite some time for their            30.____
     interview may, justifiably, become upset.
     However, a client may initially attempt to mask these
     feelings because he may
         A. personally hurt the interviewer
         B. want to be civil
         C. feel that the wait was unavoidable
         D. fear the consequences of his statement

# KEY (CORRECT ANSWERS)

| | | | | | |
|---|---|---|---|---|---|
| 1. | B | 11. | A | 21. | A |
| 2. | C | 12. | B | 22. | C |
| 3. | D | 13. | D | 23. | B |
| 4. | D | 14. | D | 24. | D |
| 5. | B | 15. | C | 25. | D |
| 6. | D | 16. | B | 26. | A |
| 7. | C | 17. | C | 27. | B |
| 8. | C | 18. | A | 28. | C |
| 9. | D | 19. | D | 29. | B |
| 10. | C | 20. | D | 30. | B |

———

# TEST 2

DIRECTIONS: Each question or incomplete statement is followed by several suggested answers or completions. Select the one that BEST answers the question or completes the statement. *PRINT THE LETTER OF THE CORRECT ANSWER IN THE SPACE AT THE RIGHT.*

Questions 1-5.

DIRECTIONS: In Questions 1 through 5, choose the sentence which is BEST from the point of view of English usage suitable for a business report.

1.  A. The client's receiving of public assistance checks at         1.___
       two different addresses were disclosed by the investi-
       gation.
    B. The investigation disclosed that the client was receiving
       public assistance checks at two different addresses.
    C. The client was found out by the investigation to be
       receiving public assistance checks at two different
       addresses.
    D. The client has been receiving public assistance checks
       at two different addresses, disclosed the investigation.

2.  A. The investigation of complaints are usually handled by      2.___
       this unit, which deals with internal security problems
       in the department.
    B. This unit deals with internal security problems in the
       department; usually investigating complaints.
    C. Investigating complaints is this unit's job, being that
       it handles internal security problems in the department.
    D. This unit deals with internal security problems in the
       department and usually investigates complaints.

3.  A. The delay in completing this investigation was caused       3.___
       by difficulty in obtaining the required documents from
       the candidate.
    B. Because of difficulty in obtaining the required docu-
       ments from the candidate is the reason that there was
       a delay in completing this investigation.
    C. Having had difficulty in obtaining the required docu-
       ments from the candidate, there was a delay in completing
       this investigation.
    D. Difficulty in obtaining the required documents from the
       candidate had the affect of delaying the completion of
       this investigation.

4.  A. This report, together with documents supporting our         4.___
       recommendation, are being submitted for your approval.
    B. Documents supporting our recommendation is being sub-
       mitted with the report for your approval.

    C. This report, together with documents supporting our
       recommendation, is being submitted for your approval.
    D. The report and documents supporting our recommendation
       is being submitted for your approval.

5.  A. Several people were interviewed and numerous letters     5.___
      were sent before this case was completed.
   B. Completing this case, interviewing several people and
      sending numerous letters were necessary.
   C. To complete this case needed interviewing several people
      and sending numerous letters.
   D. Interviewing several people and sending numerous letters
      was necessary to complete the case.

Questions 6-20.

DIRECTIONS:   For each of the sentences numbered 6 to 20, select from
                the options given below the MOST applicable choice, and
                mark your answer accordingly.

       A. The sentence is correct.
       B. The sentence contains a spelling error only.
       C. The sentence contains an English grammar error only.
       D. The sentence contains both a spelling error and an
          English grammar error.

6.  He is a very dependible person whom we expect will be an     6.___
    asset to this division.

7.  An investigator often finds it necessary to be very dip-     7.___
    lomatic when conducting an interview.

8.  Accurate detail is especially important if court action     8.___
    results from an investigation.

9.  The report was signed by him and I since we conducted the     9.___
    investigation jointly.

10.  Upon receipt of the complaint, an inquiry was begun.     10.___

11.  An employee has to organize his time so that he can     11.___
    handle his workload efficiantly.

12.  It was not apparant that anyone was living at the address     12.___
    given by the client.

13.  According to regulations, there is to be at least three     13.___
    attempts made to locate the client.

14.  Neither the inmate nor the correction officer was willing     14.___
    to sign a formal statement.

15.  It is our opinion that one of the persons interviewed     15.___
    were lying.

16. We interviewed both clients and departmental personal in    16.___
the course of this investigation.

17. It is concievable that further research might produce    17.___
additional evidence.

18. There are too many occurences of this nature to ignore.    18.___

19. We cannot accede to the candidate's request.    19.___

20. The submission of overdue reports is the reason that    20.___
there was a delay in completion of this investigation.

Questions 21-25.

DIRECTIONS:    Each of Questions 21 to 25 consists of three sentences
lettered A, B, and C. In each of these questions, one
of the sentences may contain an error in grammar, sentence structure, or punctuation, or all three sentences
may be correct. If one of the sentences in a question
contains an error in grammar, sentence structure, or
punctuation, print in the space on the right the capital
letter preceding the sentence which contains the error.
If all three sentences are correct, print the letter D.

21. A. Mr. Smith appears to be less competent than I in    21.___
performing these duties.
B. The supervisor spoke to the employee, who had made
the error, but did not reprimand him.
C. When he found the book lying on the table, he immediately notified the owner.

22. A. Being locked in the desk, we were certain that the    22.___
papers would not be taken.
B. It wasn't I who dictated the telegram; I believe it
was Eleanor.
C. You should interview whoever comes to the office today.

23. A. The clerk was instructed to set the machine on the    23.___
table before summoning the manager.
B. He said that he was not familiar with those kind of
activities.
C. A box of pencils, in addition to erasers and blotters,
was included in the shipment of supplies.

24. A. The supervisor remarked, "Assigning an employee to    24.___
the proper type of work is not always easy."
B. The employer found that each of the applicants were
qualified to perform the duties of the position.
C. Any competent student is permitted to take this course
if he obtains the consent of the instructor.

25. A. The prize was awarded to the employee whom the judges    25.___
       believed to be most deserving.
    B. Since the instructor believes this book is the better
       of the two, he is recommending it for use in the school.
    C. It was obvious to the employees that the completion of
       the task by the scheduled date would require their work-
       ing overtime.

_____

# KEY (CORRECT ANSWERS)

| | |
|---|---|
| 1. B | 11. B |
| 2. D | 12. B |
| 3. A | 13. C |
| 4. C | 14. A |
| 5. A | 15. C |
| 6. D | 16. B |
| 7. A | 17. B |
| 8. A | 18. B |
| 9. C | 19. A |
| 10. A | 20. C |

21. B
22. A
23. B
24. B
25. D

# INTERVIEWING
# EXAMINATION SECTION

DIRECTIONS FOR THIS SECTION:

Each question or incomplete statement is followed by several suggested answers or completions. Select the one that BEST answers the question or completes the statement. *PRINT THE LETTER OF THE CORRECT ANSWER IN THE SPACE AT THE RIGHT.*

# TEST 1

1. Of the following, the MAIN advantage to the supervisor of       1. ...
   using the indirect (or nondirective) interview, in which
   he asks only guiding questions and encourages the employee
   to do most of the talking, is that he can
   - A. obtain a mass of information about the employee in a
     very short period of time
   - B. easily get at facts which the employee wishes to conceal
   - C. get answers which are not slanted or biased in order to
     win his favor
   - D. effectively deal with an employee's serious emotional
     problems

2. An interviewer under your supervision routinely closes his    2. ...
   interview with a reassuring remark such as, "I'm sure you
   soon will be well," or "Everything will soon be all right."
   This practice is USUALLY considered
   - A. *advisable,* chiefly because the interviewer may make
     the patient feel better
   - B. *inadvisable,* chiefly because it may cause a patient
     who is seriously ill to doubt the worker's under-
     standing of the situation
   - C. *advisable,* chiefly because the patient becomes more
     receptive if further interviews are needed
   - D. *inadvisable,* chiefly because the interviewer should
     usually not show that he is emotionally involved

3. An interviewer has just ushered out a client he has inter-    3. ...
   viewed. As the interviewer is preparing to leave, the
   client mentions a fact that seems to contradict the in-
   formation he has given.
   Of the following, it would be BEST for the interviewer at
   this time to
   - A. make no response but write the fact down in his report
     and plan to come back another day
   - B. point out to the client that he has contradicted him-
     self and ask for an explanation
   - C. ask the client to elaborate on the comment and attempt
     to find out further information about the fact
   - D. disregard the comment since the client was probably
     exhausted and not thinking clearly

4. A client who is being interviewed insists on certain facts.   4. ...
   The interviewer knows that these statements are incorrect.
   In regard to the rest of the client's statements, the in-
   terviewer is MOST justified to
   - A. disregard any information the client gives which can-
     not be verified
   - B. try to discover other misstatements by confronting the
     client with the discrepancy
   - C. consider everything else which the client has said as
     the truth unless proved otherwise

1

D. ask the client to prove his statements
5. Immediately after the interviewer identifies himself to        5. ...
a client, she says in a hysterical voice that she is not
to be trusted.
Of the following, the BEST course of action for the interviewer to follow would be to
   A. tell the woman sternly that if she does not stay calm,
      he will leave
   B. assure the woman that there is no cause to worry
   C. ignore the woman until she becomes quiet
   D. ask the woman to explain her problem
6. Assume that you are an interviewer and that one of your        6. ...
interviewees has asked you for advice on dealing with a
personal problem.
Of the following, the BEST action for you to take is to
   A. tell him about a similar problem which you know
      worked out well
   B. advise him not to worry
   C. explain that the problem is quite a usual one and
      that the situation will be brighter soon
   D. give no opinion and change the subject when practicable
7. All of the following are, *generally*, good approaches for        7. ...
an interviewer to use in order to improve his interviews
EXCEPT
   A. developing a routine approach so that interviews can
      be standardized
   B. comparing his procedure with that of others engaged
      in similar work
   C. reviewing each interview critically, picking out one
      or two weak points to concentrate on improving
   D. comparing his own more successful and less successful
      interviews
8. Assume that a supervisor suggests at a staff meeting that        8. ...
tape recording machines be provided for interviewers.
Following are four arguments *against* the use of tape re-
corders that are raised by other members of the staff that
might be valid:
   I. Recorded interviews provide too much unnecessary in-
      formation.
  II. Recorded interviews provide no record of manner or
      gestures.
 III. Tape recorders are too cumbersome and difficult for
      the average supervisor to manage.
  IV. Tape recorders may inhibit the interviewee.
Which one of the following choices MOST accurately classi-
fies the above into those which are generally *valid* and
those which are *not?*
   A. I and II are generally valid, but III and IV are not.
   B. IV is generally valid, but I, II and III are not.
   C. I, II and IV are generally valid, but III is not.
   D. I, II, III and IV are generally valid.
9. During an interview the PRIMARY advantage of the technique        9. ...
of using questions as opposed to allowing the interviewee
to talk freely is that questioning
   A. gives the interviewer greater control
   B. provides a more complete picture

2

C. makes the interviewee more relaxed

D. decreases the opportunity for exaggeration

10. Assume that, in conducting an interview, an interviewer    10. ...
takes into consideration the age, sex, education, and
background of the subject.
This practice is GENERALLY considered
A. *undesirable*, mainly because an interviewer may be
prejudiced by such factors
B. *desirable*, mainly because these are factors which
might influence a person's response to certain questions
C. *undesirable*, mainly because these factors rarely have
any bearing on the matter being investigated
D. *desirable*, mainly because certain categories of people
answer certain questions in the same way

11. If a client should begin to tell his life story during an   11. ...
interview, the BEST course of action for an interviewer to
take is to
A. interrupt immediately and insist that they return to
business
B. listen attentively until the client finishes and then
ask if they can return to the subject
C. pretend to have other business and come back later to
see the client
D. interrupt politely at an appropriate point and direct
the client's attention to the subject

12. An interviewer who is trying to discover the circumstances  12. ...
surrounding a client's accident would be MOST successful
during an interview if he avoided questions which
A. lead the client to discuss the matter in detail
B. can easily be answered by either "yes" or "no"
C. ask for specific information
D. may be embarrassing or annoying to the client

13. A client being interviewed may develop an emotional re-    13. ...
action (positive or negative) toward the interviewer.
The BEST attitude for the interviewer to take toward
such feelings is that they are
A. *inevitable;* they should be accepted but kept under
control
B. *unusual;* they should be treated impersonally
C. *obstructive;* they should be resisted at all costs
D. *abnormal;* they should be eliminated as soon as possible

14. Encouraging the client being interviewed to talk freely   14. ...
at first is a technique that is supported by all of the
following reasons EXCEPT that it
A. tends to counteract any preconceived ideas that the
interviewer may have entertained about the client
B. gives the interviewer a chance to learn the best
method of approach to obtain additional information
C. inhibits the client from looking to the interviewer
for support and advice
D. allows the client to reveal the answers to many
questions before they are asked

15. Of the following, *generally*, the MOST effective way for   15. ...
an interviewer to assure full cooperation from the client
he is interviewing is to
A. sympathize with the client's problems and assure
him of concern

3

B. tell a few jokes before beginning to ask questions
C. convince the patient that the answers to the questions will help him as well as the interviewer
D. arrange the interview when the client feels best

16. Since many elderly people are bewildered and helpless   16. ...
when interviewed, special consideration should be given
to them.
Of the following, the BEST way for an interviewer to
*initially* approach elderly clients who express anxiety
and fear is to
A. assure them that they have nothing to worry about
B. listen patiently and show interest in them
C. point out the specific course of action that is
best for them
D. explain to them that many people have overcome much
greater difficulties

17. Assume that, in planning an initial interview, an inter-   17. ...
viewer determines in advance what information is needed
in order to fulfill the purpose of the interview.
Of the following, this procedure usually does NOT
A. reduce the number of additional interviews required
B. expedite the processing of the case
C. improve public opinion of the interviewer's agency
D. assure the cooperation of the person interviewed

18. Sometimes an interviewer deliberately introduces his own   18. ...
personal interests and opinions into an interview with a
client.
In general, this practice should be considered
A. *desirable*, primarily because the relationship between
client and interviewer becomes social rather than
businesslike
B. *undesirable*, primarily because the client might com-
plain to his supervisor
C. *desirable;* primarily because the focus of attention
is directed toward the client
D. *undesirable;* primarily because an argument between
client and interviewer could result

19. The one of the following types of interviewees who pres-   19. ...
ents the LEAST difficult problem to handle is the person
who
A. answers with a great many qualifications
B. talks at length about unrelated subjects so that the
interviewer cannot ask questions
C. has difficulty understanding the interviewer's
vocabulary
D. breaks into the middle of sentences and completes
them with a meaning of his own

20. A man being interviewed is entitled to Medicaid, but he   20. ...
refuses to sign up for it because he says he cannot accept
any form of welfare.
Of the following, the *best* course of action for an interviewer to take FIRST is to
A. try to discover the reason for his feeling this way
B. tell him that he should be glad financial help is
available

4

C. explain that others cannot help him if he will not
help himself
D. suggest that he speak to someone who is already on
Medicaid

21. Of the following, the outcome of an interview by an inter- 21. ...
viewer depends MOST heavily on the
A. personality of the interviewee
B. personality of the interviewer
C. subject matter of the questions asked
D. interaction between interviewer and interviewee

22. Some clients being interviewed by an interviewer are        22. ...
primarily interested in making a favorable impression.
The interviewer should be aware of the fact that such
clients are MORE likely than *other* clients to
A. try to anticipate the answers the interviewer is
looking for
B. answer all questions openly and frankly
C. try to assume the role of interviewer
D. be anxious to get the interview over as quickly as
possible

23. The type of interview which a hospital care interviewer     23. ...
usually conducts is *substantially different* from most
interviewing situations in all of the following aspects
EXCEPT the
A. setting                  B. kinds of clients
C. techniques employed      D. kinds of problems

24. During an interview, an interviewer uses a "leading ques-   24. ...
tion."
This type of question is so-called because it, *generally*,
A. starts a series of questions about one topic
B. suggests the answer which the interviewer wants
C. forms the basis for a following "trick" question
D. sets, at the beginning, the tone of the interview

25. An interviewer may face various difficulties when he tries  25. ...
to obtain information from a client.
Of the following, the difficulty which is EASIEST for the
interviewer to *overcome* occurs when a client
A. is unwilling to reveal the information
B. misunderstands what information is needed
C. does not have the information available to him
D. is unable to coherently give the information requested

# TEST 2

1. Of the following, the MOST appropriate manner for an in-     1. ...
terviewer to assume during an interview with a client is
A. authoritarian  B. paternal  C. casual  D. businesslike

2. The systematic study of interviewing theory, principles     2. ...
and techniques by an interviewer will, *usually*,
A. aid him to act in a depersonalized manner
B. turn his interviewes into stereotyped affairs
C. make the people he interviews feel manipulated
D. give him a basis for critically examining his own
practice

3. Compiling in advance a list of general questions to ask a     3. ...
   client during an interview is a technique *usually* considered
      A. *desirable,* chiefly because reference to the list will
         help keep the interview focused on the important issues
      B. *undesirable,* chiefly because use of such a list will
         discourage the client from speaking freely
      C. *desirable,* chiefly because the list will serve as a
         record of what questions were asked
      D. *undesirable,* chiefly because use of such a list will
         make the interview too mechanical and impersonal

4. The one of the following which is usually of GREATEST     4. ...
   importance in winning the cooperation of a person being
   interviewed while achieving the purpose of the interview
   is the interviewer's ability to
      A. gain the confidence of the person being interviewed
      B. stick to the subject of the interview
      C. handle a person who is obviously lying
      D. prevent the person being interviewed from withholding
         information

5. While interviewing clients, an interviewer should use the     5. ...
   technique of interruption, beginning to speak when a client
   has temporarily paused at the end of a phrase or sentence,
   in order to
      A. limit the client's ability to voice his objections
         or complaints
      B. shorten, terminate or redirect a client's response
      C. assert authority when he feels that the client is too
         conceited
      D. demonstrate to the client that pauses in speech should
         be avoided

6. An interviewer might gain background information about a     6. ...
   client by being aware of the person's speech during an
   interview.
   Which one of the following patterns of speech would offer
   the LEAST accurate information about a client?  The
      A. number of slang expressions and the level of vocabulary
      B. presence and degree of an accent
      C. rate of speech and the audibility level
      D. presence of a physical speech defect

7. Suppose that you are interviewing a distressed client who     7. ...
   claims that he was just laid off from his job and has no
   money to pay his rent.
   Your FIRST action should be to
      A. ask if he has sought other employment or has other
         sources of income
      B. express your sympathy but explain that he must pay
         the rent on time
      C. inquire about the reasons he was laid off from work
      D. try to transfer him to a smaller apartment which he
         can afford

8. Suppose you have some background information on an appli-     8. ...
   cant whom you are interviewing.  During the interview it
   appears that the applicant is giving you *false* information.
   The BEST thing for you to do at that point is to
      A. pretend that you are not aware of the written facts
         and let him continue

    B. tell him what you already know and discuss the dis-
       crepancies with him
    C. terminate the interview and make a note that the
       applicant is untrustworthy
    D. tell him that, because he is making false statements,
       he will not be eligible for an apartment

9. A Spanish-speaking applicant may want to bring his bilin-   9. ...
gual child with him to an interview to act as an interpreter.
Which of the following would be LEAST likely to affect the
value of an interview in which an applicant's child has
acted as interpreter?
    A. It may make it undesirable to ask certain questions.
    B. A child may do an inadequate job of interpretation.
    C. A child's answers may indicate his feelings toward
       his parents.
    D. The applicant may not want to reveal all information
       in front of his child.

10. Assume you are assigned to interview applicants.   10. ...
Of the following, which is the BEST attitude for you to
take in dealing with applicants?
    A. Assume they will enjoy being interviewed because they
       believe that you have the power of decision
    B. Expect that they have a history of anti-social behav-
       ior in the family, and probe deeply into the social
       development of family members
    C. Expect that they will try to control the interview,
       thus you should keep them on the defensive
    D. Assume that they will be polite and cooperative and
       attempt to secure the information you need in a
       business-like manner

11. If you are interviewing an applicant who is a minority   11. ...
group member in reference to his eligibility, it would
be BEST for you to use language that is
    A. *informal*, using ethnic expressions known to the
       applicant
    B. *technical*, using the expressions commonly used in
       the agency
    C. *simple*, using words and phrases which laymen understand
    D. *formal*, to remind the applicant that he is dealing with
       a government agency

12. When interviewing an applicant to determine his eligibil-  12. ...
ity, it is MOST important to
    A. have a prior mental picture of the typical eligible
       applicant
    B. conduct the interview strictly according to a previous-
       ly prepared script
    C. keep in mind the goal of the interview, which is to
       determine eligibility
    D. get an accurate and detailed account of the applicant's
       life history

13. The practice of trying to imagine yourself in the appli-  13. ...
cant's place during an interview is
    A. *good;* mainly because you will be able to evaluate his
       responses better
    B. *good;* mainly because it will enable you to treat him
       as a friend rather than as an applicant

C. *poor;* mainly because it is important for the applicant to see you as an impartial person
D. *poor;* mainly because it is too time-consuming to do this with each applicant

14. When dealing with clients from different ethnic backgrounds, you should be aware of certain tendencies toward prejudice.
Which of the following statements is LEAST likely to be valid?
  A. Whites prejudiced against blacks are more likely to be prejudiced against Puerto Ricans than whites not prejudiced against blacks.
  B. The less a white is in competition with blacks, the less likely he is to be prejudiced against them.
  C. Persons who have moved from one social group to another are likely to retain the attitudes and prejudices of their original social group.
  D. When there are few blacks or Puerto Ricans in a project, whites are less likely to be prejudiced against them than when there are many.

14. ...

15. Of the following, the one who is MOST likely to be a good interviewer of people seeking assistance, is one who
  A. tries to get applicants to apply to another agency instead
  B. believes that it is necessary to get as much pertinent information as possible in order to determine the applicant's real needs
  C. believes that people who seek assistance are likely to have persons with a history of irresponsible behavior in their households
  D. is convinced that there is no need for a request for assistance

15. ...

# KEYS (CORRECT ANSWERS)

| TEST 1 | | | | TEST 2 | |
|---|---|---|---|---|---|
| 1. | C | 11. | D | 1. | D |
| 2. | B | 12. | B | 2. | D |
| 3. | C | 13. | A | 3. | A |
| 4. | C | 14. | C | 4. | A |
| 5. | D | 15. | C | 5. | B |
| 6. | D | 16. | B | 6. | C |
| 7. | A | 17. | D | 7. | A |
| 8. | C | 18. | D | 8. | B |
| 9. | A | 19. | C | 9. | C |
| 10. | B | 20. | A | 10. | D |
| | | 21. | D | 11. | C |
| | | 22. | A | 12. | C |
| | | 23. | C | 13. | A |
| | | 24. | B | 14. | C |
| | | 25. | B | 15. | B |

# READING COMPREHENSION
## UNDERSTANDING AND INTERPRETING WRITTEN MATERIAL

DIRECTIONS FOR THIS SECTION:
   All questions are to be answered *SOLELY* on the basis of the information contained in the passage.
   Each question or incomplete statement is followed by several suggested answers or completions. Select the one that *BEST* answers the question or completes the statement. *PRINT THE LETTER OF THE CORRECT ANSWER IN THE SPACE AT THE RIGHT*.

# TEST 1

Questions 1-7.
   Snow-covered roads spell trouble for motorists all winter long. Clearing highways of snow and ice to keep millions of motor vehicles moving freely is a tremendous task. Highway departments now rely, to a great extent, on chemical de-icers to get the big job done. Sodium chloride, in the form of commercial salt, is the de-icer most frequently used.
   There is no reliable evidence to prove that salt reduces highway accidents. But available statistics are impressive. For example, before Massachusetts used chemical de-icers, it had a yearly average of 21 fatal accidents and 1,635 injuries attributed to cars skidding on snow or ice. Beginning in 1940, the state began fighting hazardous driving conditions with chemical de-icers. During the period 1940-50, there was a yearly average of only seven deaths and 736 injuries as a result of skids.
   Economical and effective in a moderately low temperature range, salt is increasingly popular with highway departments, but not so popular with individual car owners. Salty slush eats away at metal, including auto bodies. It also sprinkles windshields with a fine-grained spray which dries on contact, severely reducing visibility. However, drivers who are hindered or immobilized by heavy winter weather favor the liberal use of products such as sodium chloride. When snow blankets roads, these drivers feel that the quickest way to get back to the safety of driving on bare pavement is through use of de-icing salts.

1. The *MAIN* reason given by the above passage for the use of    1. ...
   sodium chloride as a de-icer is that it
      A. has no harmful side effects    B. is economical
      C. is popular among car owners    D. reduces highway accidents

2. The above passage may *BEST* be described as a(n)    2. ...
      A. argument against the use of sodium chloride as a de-icer
      B. discussion of some advantages and disadvantages of sodium chloride as a de-icer
      C. recommendation to use sodium chloride as a de-icer
      D. technical account of the uses and effects of sodium chloride as a de-icer

3. Based on the above passage, the use of salt on snow-    3. ...
   covered roadways will eventually
      A. decrease the efficiency of the automobile fuel
      B. cause tires to deteriorate
      C. damage the surface of the roadway
      D. cause holes in the sides of cars

4. The average number of persons killed yearly in Massachu-    4. ...
   setts in car accidents caused by skidding on snow or ice,
   before chemical de-icers were used there, was
      A. 9          B. 12          C. 21          D. 30

1

5. According to the passage, it would be advisable to use 5. ...
salt as a de-icer when
   A. outdoor temperatures are somewhat below freezing
   B. residues on highway surfaces are deemed to be undesirable
   C. snow and ice have low absorbency characteristics
   D. the use of a substance is desired which dries on contact
6. As a result of using chemical de-icers, the number of in- 6. ...
juries resulting from skids in Massachusetts was reduced
by about
   A. 35%     B. 45%     C. 55%     D. 65%
7. According to the above passage, driver visibility can be 7. ...
severely reduced by
   A. sodium chloride deposits on the windshield
   B. glare from salt and snow crystals
   C. salt spray covering the front lights
   D. faulty windshield wipers

Questions 8-10.

An employee should call the Fire Department for any fire except a small one in a wastebasket. This kind of fire can be put out with a fire extinguisher. If the employee is not sure about the size of the fire, he should not wait to find out how big it is. He should call the Fire Department at once.

Every employee should know what to do when a fire starts. He should know how to use the fire-fighting tools in the building and how to call the Fire Department. He should also know where the nearest fire alarm box is. But the most important thing for an employee to do in case of fire is to avoid panic.

8. If there is a small fire in a wastebasket, an employee 8. ...
should
   A. call the Fire Department B. let it burn itself out
   C. open a window
   D. put it out with a fire extinguisher
9. In case of fire, the most important thing for an employee 9. ...
to do is to
   A. find out how big it is  B. keep calm
   C. leave the building right away
   D. report to his boss
10. If a large fire starts while he is at work, an employee 10. ...
should *always FIRST*
   A. call the Fire Department
   B. notify the Housing Superintendent
   C. remove inflammables from the building
   D. use a fire extinguisher

Questions 11-12.

Those correction theorists who are in agreement with severe and rig controls as a normal part of the correctional process are confronted wi a contradiction; this is so because a responsibility which is consisten with freedom cannot be developed in a repressive atmosphere. They do not recognize this contradiction when they carry out their programs wit dictatorial force and expect convicted criminals exposed to such progra to be reformed into free and responsible citizens.

11. According to the above paragraph, those correction 11. ...
theorists are faced with a contradiction who
   A. are in favor of the enforcement of strict controls in a
      prison
   B. believe that to develop a sense of responsibility, free-
      dom must not be restricted
   C. take the position that the development of responsibility
      consistent with freedom is not possible in a repressive
      atmosphere

2

   D. think that freedom and responsibility can be developed
      only in a democratic atmosphere
12. According to the above paragraph, a repressive atmosphere   12. ...
    in a prison
    A. does not conform to present-day ideas of freedom of the
       individual
    B. is admitted by correction theorists to be in conflict
       with the basic principles of the normal correctional
       process
    C. is advocated as the best method of maintaining discipline
       when rehabilitation is of secondary importance
    D. is not suitable for the development of a sense of re-
       sponsibility consistent with freedom
Questions 13-16.
   Abandoned cars - with tires gone, chrome stripped away, and
windows smashed - have become a common sight on the City's streets.
In 1970, more than 72,000 were deposited at curbs by owners who never
came back, an increase of 15,000 from the year before and more than
30 times the number abandoned a decade ago.  In January, 1971, the
City's Environmental Protection Administrator asked the State Legislature to pass a law requiring a buyer of a new automobile to deposit
$100 and an owner of an automobile at the time the law takes effect to
deposit $50 with the State Department of Motor Vehicles.  In return,
they would be given a certificate of deposit which would be passed on
to each succeeding owner.  The final owner would get the deposit money
back if he could present proof that he has disposed of his car "in an
environmentally acceptable manner."  The Legislature has given no
indication that it plans to rush ahead on the matter.
13. The number of cars abandoned in City streets in 1960 was,   13. ...
    most nearly,
    A. 2,500      B. 12,000      C. 27,500      D. 57,000
14. The proposed law would require a person who owned a car      14. ...
    bought before the law was passed to deposit
    A. $100 with the State Department of Motor Vehicles
    B. $50 with the Environmental Protection Administration
    C. $100 with the State Legislature
    D. $50 with the State Department of Motor Vehicles
15. The proposed law would require the State to return the       15. ...
    deposit money *only when* the
    A. original owner of the car shows proof that he sold it
    B. last owner of the car shows proof that he got rid of
       the car in a satisfactory way
    C. owner of a car shows proof that he has transferred the
       certificate of deposit to the next owner
    D. last owner of a car returns the certificate of deposit
16. The *main* idea or theme of the above article is that        16. ...
    A. a proposed new law would make it necessary for car
       owners in the State to pay additional taxes
    B. the State Legislature is against a proposed law to
       require deposits from automobile owners to prevent
       them from abandoning their cars
    C. the City is trying to find a solution for the increas-
       ing number of cars abandoned on its streets
    D. to pay for the removal of abandoned cars, the City's
       Environmental Protection Administrator has asked the
       State to fine automobile owners who abandon their
       vehicles

3

Questions 17-19.

The German roach is the most common roach in houses in the United States. Adults are pale brown and about 1/2-inch long; both sexes have wings as long as the body, and can be distinguished from other roaches by the two dark stripes on the pronotum. The female carries its egg capsule protruding from her abdomen until the eggs are ready to hatch. This is the only common house-infesting species which carries the egg capsule for such an extended period of time. A female will usually produce 4 to 8 capsules in her lifetime. Each capsule contains 30 to 48 eggs which hatch out in about 28 days at ordinary room temperature. The completion of the nymphal stage under room conditions requires 40 to 125 days. German roaches may live as adults for as long as 303 days.

It is stated about that the German cockroach is the most commonly encountered of the house-infesting species in the United States. The reasons for this are somewhat complex, but the understanding of some of the factors involved are basic to the practice of pest control. In the first place, the German cockroach has a larger number of eggs per capsule and a shorter hatching time than do the other species. It also requires a shorter period from hatching until sexual maturity, so that within a given period of time a population of German roaches will produce a larger number of eggs. On the basis of this fact, we can state that this species has a high reproductive potential. Since the female carries the egg capsule during nearly the entire time that the embryos are developing within the egg, many hazards of the environment which may affect the eggs are avoided. This means that more nymphs are likely to hatch and that a larger portion of the reproductive potential is realized. The nymphs which hatch from each egg capsule tend to stay close to each other, and since they are often close to the female at time of hatching, there is a tendency for the population density to be high locally. Being smaller than most of the other roaches, they are able to conceal themselves in many places which are inaccessible to individuals of the larger species. All of these factors combined help to give the German cockroach an advantage with regard to group survival.

17. According to the above passage, the *most important*       17. ...
    feature of the German roach which gives it an advantage
    over other roaches is its
    A. distinctive markings       B. immunity to disease
    C. long life span             D. power to reproduce
18. An *important* difference between an adult female German       18. ...
    roach and an adult female of other species is the
    A. black bars or stripes which appear on the abdomen
       of the German roach
    B. German roach's preference for warm, moi  places
       in which to breed
    C. long period of time during which the German roach
       carries the egg capsule
    D. presence of longer wings on the female German roach
19. A storeroom in a certain housing project has an infesta-       19. ...
    tion of German roaches, which includes 125 adult female.
    If the infestation is not treated and ordinary room
    temperature is maintained in the storeroom, *how many*
    eggs will hatch out during the lifetime of these females
    if they each lay 8 capsules containing 48 eggs each?
    A. 1,500       B. 48,000       C. 96,000       D. 303,000

4

Questions 20-22.

City governments have long had building codes which set minimum standards for building and for human occupancy. The code (or series of codes) makes provisions for standards of lighting and ventilation, sanitation, fire prevention, and protection. As a result of demands from manufacturers, builders, real estate people, tenement owners, and building-trades unions, these codes often have established minimum standards well below those that the contemporary society would accept as a rock-bottom minimum. Codes often become outdated, so that meager standards in one era become seriously inadequate a few decades later as society's concept of a minimum standard of living changes. Out-of-date codes, when still in use, have sometimes prevented the introduction of new devices and modern building techniques. Thus, it is extremely important that building codes keep pace with changes in the accepted concept of a minimum standard of living.

20. According to the above passage, all of the following con-    20. ...
    siderations in building planning would probably be covered
    in a building code *EXCEPT*
    A. closet space as a percentage of total floor area
    B. size and number of windows required for rooms of dif-
       fering sizes
    C. placement of fire escapes in each line of apartments
    D. type of garbage disposal units to be installed
21. According to the above passage, if an ideal building code    21. ...
    were to be created, *how* would the established minimum
    standards in it compare to the ones that are presently
    set by city governments? They would
    A. *be lower* than they are at present
    B. *be higher* than they are at present
    C. *be comparable* to the present minimum standards
    D. *vary* according to the economic group that sets them
22. On the basis of the above passage, *what* is the reason    22. ...
    for difficulties in introducing new building techniques?
    A. Builders prefer techniques which represent the rock-
       bottom minimum desired by society.
    B. Certain manufacturers have obtained patents on various
       building methods to the exclusion of new techniques.
    C. The government does not want to invest money in tech-
       niques that will soon be outdated.
    D. New techniques are not provided for in building codes
       which are not up to date.

Questions 23-25.

A flameproof fabric is defined as one which, when exposed to small sources of ignition such as sparks or smoldering cigarettes, does not burn beyond the vicinity of the source of the ignition. Cotton fabrics are the materials commonly used that are considered most hazardous. Other materials, such as acetate rayons and linens, are somewhat less hazardous, and woolens and some natural silk fabrics, even when untreated, are about the equal of the average treated cotton fabric insofar as flame spread and ease of ignition are concerned. The method of application is to immerse the fabric in a flameproofing solution. The container used must be large enough so that all the fabric is thoroughly wet and there are no folds which the solution does not penetrate.

23. According to the above paragraph, a flameproof fabric is    23. ...
one which
A. is unaffected by heat and smoke
B. resists the spread of flames when ignited
C. burns with a cold flame
D. cannot be ignited by sparks or cigarettes
E. may smolder but cannot burn
24. According to the above paragraph, woolen fabrics which    24. ...
have not been flameproofed are as likely to catch fire as
A. treated silk fabrics    B. treated acetate rayon fabrics
C. untreated linen fabrics
D. untreated synthetic fabrics
E. treated cotton fabrics
25. In the method described above, the flameproofing solution    25. ...
is *BEST* applied to the fabric by
A. sponging the fabric    B. spraying the fabric
C. dipping the fabric    D. brushing the fabric
E. sprinkling the fabric

# TEST 2

Questions 1-4.
Safety belts provide protection for the passengers of a vehicle
by preventing them from crashing around inside if the vehicle is
involved in a collision. They operate on the principle similar to
that used in the packaging of fragile items. You become a part of
the vehicle package and you are kept from being tossed about inside
if the vehicle is suddenly decelerated. Many injury-causing col-
lisions at low speeds - for example, at city intersections - could
have been injury-free if the occupants had fastened their safety
belts. There is a double advantage to the driver in that it not
only protects him from harm, but prevents him from being yanked away
from the wheel, thereby permitting him to maintain control of the
car. Since, without seat belts, the risk of injury is about 50%
greater, and the risk of death is about 30% greater, the State
Vehicle and Traffic Law provides that a motor vehicle manufactured
or assembled after June 30, 1964 and designated as a 1965 or later
model should have two safety belts for the front seat. It also provides that a motor vehicle manufactured after June 30, 1966 and
designated as a 1967 or later model should have at least one safety
belt for the rear seat for each passenger for which the rear seat of
such vehicle was designed.
1. The principle on which seat belts work is that    1. ...
A. a car and its driver and passengers are fragile
B. a person fastened to the car will not be thrown around
when the car slows down suddenly
C. the driver and passengers of a car that is suddenly
decelerated will be thrown forward
D. the driver and passengers of an automobile should be
packaged the way fragile items are packaged
2. We can assume from the above passage that safety belts    2. ...
should be worn at all times because you can never tell when
A. a car will be forced to turn off onto another road
B. it will be necessary to shift into low gear to go up
a hill

6

    C. you will have to speed up to pass another car
    D. a car may have to come to a sudden stop
3. Besides preventing injury, an *additional* benefit from     3. ...
   the use of safety belts is that
    A. collisions are fewer
    B. damage to the car is kept down
    C. the car can be kept under control
    D. the number of accidents at city intersections is re-
       duced
4. The risk of death in car accidents for people who don't    4. ...
   use safety belts is
    A. 30% greater than the risk of injury
    B. 30% greater than for those who do use them
    C. 50% less than the risk of injury
    D. 50% greater than for those who use them
Questions 5-9.
    Any person who is living in New York City and is otherwise eligible
may be granted public assistance whether or not he has New York State
residence. However, since New York City does not contribute to the
cost of assistance granted to persons who are without State residence,
the cases of all recipients must be formally identified as to whether
or not each member of the household has State residence.
    To acquire State residence a person must have resided in New York
State continuously for one year. Such residence is not lost unless
the person is out of the State continuously for a period of one year
or longer. Continuous residence does not include any period during
which the individual is a patient in a hospital, an inmate of a public
institution or of an incorporated private institution, a resident on
a military reservation, or a minor residing in a boarding home while
under the care of an authorized agency. Receipt of public assistance
does not prevent a person from acquiring State residence. State
residence, once acquired, is not lost because of absence from the
State while a person is serving in the U. S. Armed Forces or the
Merchant Marine; nor does a member of the family of such a person
lose State residence while living with or near that person in these
circumstances.
    Each person, regardless of age, acquires or loses State residence
as an individual. There is no derivative State residence except for
an infant at the time of birth. He is deemed to have State residence
if he is in the custody of both parents and either one of them has
State residence, or if the parent having custody of him has State
residence.
5. According to the above passage, an infant is deemed to     5. ...
   have New York State residence at the time of his birth if
    A. he is born in New York State but neither of his parents
       is a resident
    B. he is in the custody of only one parent, who is not a
       resident, but his other parent is a resident
    C. his brother and sister are residents
    D. he is in the custody of both his parents but only one
       of them is a resident
6. The Jones family consists of five members. Jack and Mary   6. ...
   Jones have lived in New York State continuously for the past
   eighteen months after having lived in Ohio since they were
   born. Of their three children, one was born ten months ago
   and has been in the custody of his parents since birth.

Their second child lived in Ohio until six months ago and
then moved in with his parents. Their third child had
never lived in New York until he moved with his parents
to New York eighteen months ago. However, he entered the
armed forces one month later and has not lived in New York
since that time.
Based on the above passage, how many members of the Jones
family are New York State residents?
    A. 2        B. 3        C. 4        D. 5

7. Assuming that each of the following individuals has lived    7. ...
continuously in New York State for the past year, and
has never previously lived in the State, *which one* of
them is a New York State resident?
    A. Jack Salinas, who has been an inmate in a State cor-
       rectional facility for six months of the year
    B. Fran Johnson, who has lived on an Army base for the
       entire year
    C. Arlene Snyder, who married a non-resident during the
       past year
    D. Gary Phillips, who was a patient in a Veterans Ad-
       ministration hospital for the entire year

8. The above passage implies that the reason for determining    8. ...
whether or not a recipient of public assistance is a State
resident is that
    A. the cost of assistance for non-residents is not a
       New York City responsibility
    B. non-residents living in New York City are not eligible
       for public assistance
    C. recipients of public assistance are barred from
       acquiring State residence
    D. New York City is responsible for the full cost of
       assistance to recipients who are residents

9. Assume that the Rollins household in New York City con-    9. ...
sists of six members at the present time - Anne Rollins,
her three children, her aunt, and her uncle. Anne Rollins
and one of her children moved to New York City seven months
ago. Neither of them had previously lived in New York State.
Her other two children have lived in New York City continuously for the past two years, as has her aunt. Anne Rollins'
uncle had lived in New York City continuously for many years
until two years ago. He then entered the armed forces and
has returned to New York City within the past month.
Based on the above passage, how many members of the Rollins'
household are New York State residents?
    A. 2        B. 3        C. 4        D. 6

Questions 10-12.
    The agreement under which a tenant rents property from a landlord
is known as a lease. Generally speaking, leases are classified as
either short-term or long-term in duration. They are further sub-
divided according to the method used to determine the amount of
periodic rent payments. Of the many types of lease in use, the more
commonly used ones are the following:
    1. The straight or fixed lease is one in which rent may be paid
       in equal amounts throughout the duration of the lease. These
       are usually restricted to short-term leasing, or somewhat

longer-term if clauses in the lease provide for periodic escalation of payments as the economy shifts.

2. Percentage leasing, used for short-term commercial leasing, provides the landlord with a stipulated percentage of a tenant's gross sales from goods and services sold on the premises, in addition to a fixed amount of rent.

3. The net lease, generally long-term (ten years or more), requires the tenant to pay all operating costs, including real estate taxes and insurance. In a net-net lease, the tenant further agrees to meet mortgage interest and principal payments.

4. An escalated lease, which is a long-term lease, requires rent to be of a stipulated base amount which periodically is subject to escalation in accordance with cost-of-living index scales, or in direct proportion to taxes, insurance, and operating costs.

10. Based on the information given in the passage, *which* type       10. ...
of lease is *most likely* to be advantageous to a landlord
if there is a high rate of inflation?
   A. Fixed lease                B. Percentage lease
   C. Net lease                  D. Escalated lease

11. On the basis of the above passage, *which* types of lease       11. ...
would generally be *MOST* suitable for a well-established
textile company which requires permanent facilities for
its large operations?
   A. Percentage lease and escalated lease
   B. Escalated lease and net lease
   C. Straight lease and net lease
   D. Straight lease and percentage lease

12. According to the above passage, the *only* type of lease       12. ...
which assures the same amount of rent throughout a specified interval is the
   A. straight lease             B. percentage lease
   C. net-net lease              D. escalated lease

Questions 13-18.

Basic to every office is the need for proper lighting. Inadequate lighting is a familiar cause of fatigue and serves to create a some- what dismal atmosphere in the office. One requirement of proper lighting is that it be of an appropriate intensity. Intensity is measured in foot-candles. According to the Illuminating Engineering Society of New York, for casual seeing tasks such as in reception rooms, inactive file rooms, and other service areas, it is recom- mended that the amount of light be 30 foot-candles. For ordinary seeing tasks such as reading and work in active file rooms and in mail rooms, the recommended lighting is 100 foot-candles. For very difficult seeing tasks such as accounting, transcribing, and business- machine use, the recommended lighting is 150 foot-candles.

Lighting intensity is only one requirement. Shadows and glare are to be avoided. For example, the larger the proportion of a ceiling filled with lighting units, the more glare-free and comfortable the lighting will be. Natural lighting from windows is not too dependable because on dark wintry days windows yield little usable light, and on sunny, summer afternoons the glare from windows may be very distract- ing. Desks should not face the windows. Finally, the main lighting source ought to be overhead and to the left of the user.

13. According to the above passage, insufficient light in       13. ...
the office may cause
   A. glare        B. shadows        C. tiredness    D. distraction

14. Based on the above passage, *which* of the following must   14. ...
  be considered when planning lighting arrangements? The
    A. amount of natural light present
    B. amount of work to be done
    C. level of difficulty of work to be done
    D. type of activity to be carried out
15. It can be inferred from the above passage that a well-   15. ...
  coordinated lighting scheme is likely to result in
    A. greater employee productivity
    B. elimination of light reflection
    C. lower lighting cost
    D. more use of natural light
16. Of the following, the *BEST* title for the above passage is: 16. ...
    A. Characteristics of Light B. Light Measurement Devices
    C. Factors to Consider When Planning Lighting Systems
    D. Comfort vs. Cost When Devising Lighting Arrangements
17. According to the above passage, a foot-candle is a   17. ...
  measurement of the
    A. number of bulbs used     B. strength of the light
    C. contrast between glare and shadow
    D. proportion of the ceiling filled with lighting units
18. According to the above passage, the number of foot-   18. ...
  candles of light that would be needed to copy figures
  onto a payroll is
    A. less than 30 foot-candles   B. 30 foot-candles
    C. 100 foot-candles     D. 150 foot-candles

Questions 19-22.

    A summons is an official statement ordering a person to appear in court. In traffic violation situations, summonses are used when arrests need not be made. The main reason for traffic summonses is to deter motorists from repeating the same traffic violation. Occasionally, motorists may make unintentional driving errors and sometimes they are unaware of correct driving regulations. In cases such as these, the policy should be to have the Officer verbally inform the motorist of the violation and warn him against repeating it. The purpose of this practice is not to limit the number of summonses, but rather to prevent the issuing of summonses when the violation is not due to deliberate intent or to inexcusable negligence.

19. According to the above passage, the *PRINCIPAL* reason   19. ...
  for issuing traffic summonses is to
    A. discourage motorists from violating these laws again
    B. increase the money collected by the city
    C. put traffic violators in prison
    D. have them serve as substitutes for police officers
20. The reason a verbal warning may sometimes be substituted   20. ...
  for a summons is to
    A. limit the number of summonses
    B. distinguish between excusable and inexcusable violations
    C. provide harsher penalties for deliberate intent than
      for inexcusable negligence
    D. decrease the caseload in the courts
21. The author of the above passage feels that someone who   21. ...
  violated a traffic regulation because he did *not* know
  about the regulation should be
    A. put under arrest     B. fined less money
    C. given a summons     D. told not to do it again

22. Using the distinctions made by the author of the above     22. ...
    passage, the *one* of the following motorists to whom it
    would be *MOST* desirable to issue a summons is the one
    who exceeded the speed limit because he
    A. did not know the speed limit
    B. was late for an important business appointment
    C. speeded to avoid being hit by another car
    D. had a speedometer which was not working properly
Questions 23-25.
    Physical design plays a very significant role in crime rate.
Crime rate has been found to increase almost proportionately with
building height.  The average number of crimes is much greater in
higher buildings than in lower ones (equal to or less than six stories).
What is most interesting is that in buildings of six stories or less,
the project size or total number of units does not make a difference.
It seems that, although larger projects encourage crime by fostering
feelings of anonymity, isolation, irresponsibility, and lack of identity with surroundings, evidence indicates that larger projects encom-
passed in low buildings seem to offset what we may assume to be factors
conducive to high crime rates.  High-rise projects not only experience
a higher rate of crime within the buildings, but a greater proportion
of the crime occurs in the interior public spaces of these buildings
as compared with those of the lower buildings.  Lower buildings have
more limited public space than higher ones.  A criminal probably per-
ceives that the interior public areas of buildings are where his
victims are most vulnerable and where the possibility of his being
seen or apprehended is minimal.  Placement of elevators, entrance lob-
bies, fire stairs and secondary exits all are factors related to the
likelihood of crimes taking place in buildings.  The study of all of
these elements should bear some weight in the planning of new projects.
23. According to the passage, *which* of the following *BEST*     23. ...
    describes the relationship between building size and
    crime?
    A. Larger projects lead to a greater crime rate
    B. Higher buildings tend to increase the crime rate
    C. The smaller the number of project apartments in
       low buildings the higher the crime rate
    D. Anonymity and isolation serve to lower the crime
       rate in small buildings
24. According to the passage, the likelihood of a criminal     24. ...
    attempting a mugging in the interior public portions of
    a high-rise building is good because
    A. tenants will be constantly flowing in and out of the
       area
    B. there is easy access to fire stairs and secondary
       exits
    C. there is a good chance that no one will see him
    D. tenants may not recognize the victims of crime as
       their neighbors
25. *Which* of the following is *implied* by the passage as an     25. ...
    explanation for the fact that the crime rate is lower in
    large low-rise housing projects than in large high-rise
    projects?
    A. Tenants know each other better and take a greater
       interest in what happens in the project

B. There is more public space where tenants are likely to gather together
C. The total number of units in a low-rise project is fewer than the total number of units in a high-rise project
D. Elevators in low-rise buildings travel quickly, thus limiting the amount of time in which a criminal can act

# KEYS (CORRECT ANSWERS)

## TEST 1

| | | | |
|---|---|---|---|
| 1. B | 11. A | |
| 2. B | 12. D | |
| 3. D | 13. A | |
| 4. C | 14. D | |
| 5. A | 15. B | |
| 6. C | 16. C | |
| 7. A | 17. D | |
| 8. D | 18. C | |
| 9. B | 19. B | |
| 10. A | 20. A | |

21. B
22. D
23. B
24. E
25. C

## TEST 2

| | |
|---|---|
| 1. B | 11. B |
| 2. D | 12. A |
| 3. C | 13. C |
| 4. B | 14. D |
| 5. D | 15. A |
| 6. B | 16. C |
| 7. C | 17. B |
| 8. A | 18. D |
| 9. C | 19. A |
| 10. D | 20. B |

21. D
22. B
23. B
24. C
25. A

12

# PREPARING WRITTEN MATERIAL
# PARAGRAPH REARRANGEMENT

## COMMENTARY

A type of question given on many examinations is the scrambled paragraph, or arranging sentences in "proper" order. The paragraphs which you will see will contain 4 or 5 sentences which may or may not be jumbled. Your responsibility will be to arrange them in proper order.

Most paragraphs will contain one central thought or topic. For the most part, this main thought will be expressed in the opening sentence. However, there is no rule which requires this kind of construction.

This TOPIC SENTENCE may do one of two things:

1) It may announce the subject to be discussed. This lets you know immediately what the paragraph is about.

2) It may state the writer's attitude toward his subject - tell how he feels about it.

From this point (The TOPIC SENTENCE), the remaining sentences should appear in a clear and logical order. This does NOT present a difficult problem when a paragraph describes HOW TO DO something. The order in this case is usually CHRONOLOGICAL.

However, when the objective of the paragraph is to give information or to persuade someone, the logical order becomes more difficult to perceive.

H I N T S:

1. All sentences pertaining to the same idea will usually be kept together.

2. Ideas which are necessary for a full understanding of the paragraph will appear EARLY in the paragraph.

3. Connecting language should be looked for so that you can determine which sentence (or sentences) *logically* flows from another sentence.

4. Final sentences may summarize or conclude. They may be introduced by language such as "consequently," "in conclusion," "therefore."

5. If one sentence uses a NOUN as the subject, and another sentence uses a PRONOUN for the same subject, the NOUN subject will usually PRECEDE the PRONOUN subject. e.g.: JOHN drove the CAR. HE drove IT fast.

6. TRANSITIONAL EXPRESSIONS may be used to move smoothly from one idea to another. Some of these expressions are:

| he | they | that | those | it |
| his | this | these | them | |

These words refer back to a person or an idea just mentioned. Therefore, you will have to link these sentences with a PRIOR sentence in the paragraph. They will NOT *ordinarily* be contained in the opening sentence.

7. There are certain words or expressions which CONNECT ideas in the paragraph. Some of them are:

| accordingly | for example | next |
| again | for instance | on the contrary |
| also | furthermore | on the other hand |
| although | hence | otherwise |
| as a result | however | second |
| at last | in addition | similarly |
| at the same time | in conclusion | since |
| besides | in fact | then |
| consequently | in short | therefore |
| equally important | likewise | thus |
| finally | moreover | too (also) |
| first | nevertheless | whereas |

When these expressions are used, they will indicate that one sentence is CONNECTED to a sentence that precedes it. They will NOT *usually* be used in the opening sentence.

## SAMPLE QUESTIONS

Now try to rearrange the following paragraphs. Note the underlined key words in the first example and make a conscious effort to tie the thoughts together *logically*.

1. (1) A <u>wave</u> has height from trough to crest.                          1.____
   (2) <u>It</u> has length, the distance from its crest to that of the following wave.
   (3) Before constructing an imaginary life history of a typical wave, we need to become familiar with some of its <u>physical characteristics</u>.
   (4) The period of the wave refers to the time required for succeeding crests to pass a fixed point.
       A. 1-2-3-4        B. 4-3-2-1
       C. 3-2-1-4        D. 3-1-2-4

SOLUTION TO # 1
The idea of the paragraph is to describe some physical characteristics of a WAVE. This thought is contained in sentence #3. We choose this then as our first sentence and thus eliminate choices A and B from consideration.

Sentences #1 and #2 give us true PHYSICAL CHARACTERISTICS, HEIGHT AND LENGTH. But which comes first? In sentence #1 the noun WAVE is used while in sentence #2 the pronoun IT is used. Therefore, #1 must precede #2.

The only choice which starts with #3 and has #1 preceding #2 is choice D. When we look back at the paragraph we see that sentence #4 does not truly give us a PHYSICAL CHARACTERISTIC of a WAVE, but gives us a TIME PERIOD. Our answer, then is D. 3-1-2-4.

2. (1) If your favorite uncle is a police officer, maybe you     2.____
       will make a good police officer too - but not neces-
       sarily.
   (2) Sometimes young people make the mistake of picking a
       job just because a much admired relative or friend
       likes that job.
   (3) It is risky to choose an occupation just because you
       admire or are fond of someone who has chosen it.
   (4) You may admire Joe Namath, or F. Lee Bailey, or a good
       homicide detective.
   (5) But this does not mean that you can count on being
       successful or happy as a professional ball-player,
       criminal lawyer, or famous detective.
              A. 1-2-3-4-5              B. 3-5-1-2-4
              C. 3-5-4-2-1              D. 2-1-3-4-5


SOLUTION TO #2:
As you looked at this paragraph, it became apparent that the opening sentence was not as easy to choose. Obviously, it is a choice between #2 and #3. In cases such as this, choose the sentence which seems to be broader - in this case, sentence #2. We can now disregard choices A, B and C, but not with absolute certainty.

NOTE WELL: When you have a difficult time choosing the first sentence, try to locate the concluding sentence.

Logic tells us that #5 should be last. We need to go no further. The only choice whish has #5 last and either #2 or #3 first is D. That is our answer: 2-1-3-4-5.

3. (1) The objective of the program was to relieve the ten-     3.____
       sions caused by hard studying and to meet the need of
       many students to learn to use their bodies effectively
       in trained ways.
   (2) Each location played one sport for a week, by turns for
       four weeks.
   (3) In the afternoon during the school year, all students
       at P.T.S. were required to participate in an athletic
       program.
   (4) The sports were tennis, baseball, track and soccer.

(5) Each location had one week of coaching by competent
coaches.
    A. 1-2-3-4-5        B. 3-1-4-2-5
    C. 3-1-2-4-5        D. 3-2-1-4-5

SOLUTION TO #3:

In this grouping, there is no problem choosing sentence #3 as
the first sentence. Unfortunately, we can only eliminate one
choice, A. Using straight common sense, #3 must be followed by
#1, since #3 speaks of an ATHLETIC PROGRAM and #1 gives us the
program's objectives.

Our choice is narrowed to either C or B. Again, using common
sense, #2 should precede #4. Our answer then is C. 3-1-2-4-5.

4. (1) They are words from special fields in which he has no  4.____
       contact.
  (2) While the largest English dictionaries contain over a
       million words, the average adult is said to have a use
       and recognition vocabulary of between thirty and sixty
       thousand words.
  (3) This means that nine out of ten words recognized by the
       present day official language are as strange to him as
       though they formed part of a foreign tongue.
  (4) Fortunately, he hardly ever misses them.
  (5) A highly literate adult is not likely to go much beyond
       one hundred thousand.
    A. 2-3-1-5-4        B. 2-1-5-3-4
    C. 2-5-3-1-4        D. 2-5-4-1-3

SOLUTION TO #4:

You should not have difficulty choosing sentence #2 as the
opening sentence.

Sentence #2 speaks of the number of words in the AVERAGE adult's
vocabulary. Logically following this, as a comparison, should be
the sentence which tells us how many words are in the ABOVE
AVERAGE (highly literate) adult's vocabulary - #5. Our sequence,
then, starts with 2-5. We can now eliminate choices A & B.
Choosing the next sentence is difficult, but logical, Since the
dictionary is said to contain over a million words, and the highly
literate adult understands 100,000 of these, there must be 9 out
of 10 words that are unfamiliar even to the highly literate. Therefore, choice #3 is next, and our sequence is 2-5-3 so far. We can
stop there and pick our answer as C.

But let's go further. Sentence #1 must follow #3 since it tells
us what words the highly literate adult does not understand. #4
is a tongue in cheek concluding sentence. 2-5-3-1-4.

The tests that follow contain sentences that are in scrambled order.
You are to rearrange them in proper order and indicate the letter
choice containing the correct answer in the space at the right

# EXAMINATION SECTION

DIRECTIONS: Each question consists of several sentences which can be arranged in a logical sequence. For each question, select the choice which places the numbered sentences in the MOST logical sequence. *PRINT THE LETTER OF THE CORRECT ANSWER IN THE SPACE AT THE RIGHT.*

1.      I. A body was found in the woods.                  1.___
     II. A man proclaimed innocence.
   III. The owner of a gun was located.
    IV. A gun was traced.
     V. The owner of a gun was questioned.

The CORRECT answer is:
   A. IV, III, V, II, I       B. II, I, IV, III, V
   C. I, IV, III, V, II       D. I, III, V, II, IV
   E. I, II, IV, III, V

2.      I. A man was in a hunting accident.        2.___
     II. A man fell down a flight of steps.
   III. A man lost his vision in one eye.
    IV. A man broke his leg.
     V. A man had to walk with a cane.

The CORRECT answer is:
   A. II, IV, V, I, III      B. IV, V, I, III, II
   C. III, I, IV, V, II      D. I, III, V, II, IV
   E. I, III, II, IV, V

3.      I. A man is offered a new job.          3.___
     II. A woman is offered a new job.
   III. A man works as a waiter.
    IV. A woman works as a waitress.
     V. A woman gives notice.

The CORRECT answer is:
   A. IV, II, V, III, I      B. IV, II, V, I, III
   C. II, IV, V, III, I      D. III, I, IV, II, V
   E. IV, III, II, V, I

4.      I. A train left the station late.        4.___
     II. A man was late for work.
   III. A man lost his job.
    IV. Many people complained because the train was late.
     V. There was a traffic jam.

The CORRECT answer is:
   A. V, II, I, IV, III      B. V, I, IV, II, III
   C. V, I, II, IV, III      D. I, V, IV, II, III
   E. II, I, IV, V, III

5.　I. The burden of proof as to each issue is determined　5.___
before trial and remains upon the same party throughout the trial.
II. The jury is at liberty to believe one witness' testimony as against a number of contradictory witnesses.
III. In a civil case, the party bearing the burden of proof
is required to prove his contention by a fair preponderance of the evidence.
IV. However, it must be noted that a fair preponderance
of evidence does not necessarily mean a greater
number of witnesses.
V. The burden of proof is the burden which rests upon
one of the parties to an action to persuade the trier
of the facts, generally the jury, that a proposition
he asserts is true.
VI. If the evidence is equally balanced, or if it leaves
the jury in such doubt as to be unable to decide the
controversy either way, judgment must be given
against the party upon whom the burden of proof rests.

The CORRECT answer is:
A. III, II, V, IV, I, VI　　B. I, II, VI, V, III, IV
C. III, IV, V, I, II, VI　　D. V, I, III, VI, IV, II
E. I, V, III, VI, IV, II

6.　I. If a parent is without assets and is unemployed, he　6.___
cannot be convicted of the crime of non-support of
a child.
II. The term *sufficient ability* has been held to mean
sufficient financial ability.
III. It does not matter if his unemployment is by choice
or unavoidable circumstances.
IV. If he fails to take any steps at all, he may be
liable to prosecution for endangering the welfare
of a child.
V. Under the penal law, a parent is responsible for the
support of his minor child only if the parent is *of
sufficient ability*.
VI. An indigent parent may meet his obligation by borrow-
ing money or by seeking aid under the provisions of
the Social Welfare Law.

The CORRECT answer is:
A. VI, I, V, III, II, IV　　B. I, III, V, II, IV, VI
C. V, II, I, III, VI, IV　　D. I, VI, IV, V, II, III
E. II, V, I, III, VI, IV

7.　I. Consider, for example, the case of a rabble rouser　7.___
who urges a group of twenty people to go out and
break the windows of a nearby factory.
II. Therefore, the law fills the indicated gap with the
crime of *inciting to riot*.
III. A person is considered guilty of inciting to riot
when he urges ten or more persons to engage in
tumultuous and violent conduct of a kind likely to
create public alarm.

IV. However, if he has not obtained the cooperation of at least four people, he cannot be charged with unlawful assembly.
  V. The charge of inciting to riot was added to the law to cover types of conduct which cannot be classified as either the crime of *riot* or the crime of *unlawful assembly*.
VI. If he acquires the acquiescence of at least four of them, he is guilty of unlawful assembly even if the project does not materialize.

The CORRECT answer is:
  A. III, V, I, VI, IV, II    B. V, I, IV, VI, II, III
  C. III, IV, I, V, II, VI    D. V, I, IV, VI, III, II
  E. V, III, I, VI, IV, II

8.   I. If, however, the rebuttal evidence presents an issue of credibility, it is for the jury to determine whether the presumption has, in fact, been destroyed.
  II. Once sufficient evidence to the contrary is introduced, the presumption disappears from the trial.
III. The effect of a presumption is to place the burden upon the adversary to come forward with evidence to rebut the presumption.
IV. When a presumption is overcome and ceases to exist in the case, the fact or facts which gave rise to the presumption still remain.
  V. Whether a presumption has been overcome is ordinarily a question for the court.
VI. Such information may furnish a basis for a logical inference.

The CORRECT answer is:
  A. IV, VI, II, V, I, III    B. III, II, V, I, IV, VI
  C. V, III, VI, IV, II, I    D. V, IV, I, II, VI, III
  E. II, III, V, I, IV, VI

9.   I. An executive may answer a letter by writing his reply on the face of the letter itself instead of having a return letter typed.
  II. This procedure is efficient because it saves the executive's time, the typist's time, and saves office file space.
III. Copying machines are used in small offices as well as large offices to save time and money in making brief replies to business letters.
IV. A copy is made on a copying machine to go into the company files, while the original is mailed back to the sender.

The CORRECT answer is:
  A. I, II, IV, III    B. I, IV, II, III
  C. III, I, IV, II    D. III, IV, II, I

10.      I. Most organizations favor one of the types but always    10.___
            include the others to a lesser degree.
        II. However, we can detect a definite trend toward
            greater use of symbolic control.
       III. We suggest that our local police agencies are today
            primarily utilizing material control.
        IV. Control can be classified into three types:  physical,
            material, and symbolic.

     The CORRECT answer is:
        A. IV, II, III, I              B. II, I, IV, III
        C. III, IV, II, I              D. IV, I, III, II

11.      I. Project residents had first claim to this use,         11.___
            followed by surrounding neighborhood children.
        II. By contrast, recreation space within the project's
            interior was found to be used more often by both
            groups.
       III. Studies of the use of project grounds in many cities
            showed grounds left open for public use were neglected
            and unused, both by residents and by members of the
            surrounding community.
        IV. Project residents had clearly laid claim to the play
            spaces, setting up and enforcing unwritten rules for
            use.
         V. Each group, by experience, found their activities
            easily disrupted by other groups, and their claim to
            the use of space for recreation difficult to enforce.

     The CORRECT answer is:
        A. IV, V, I, II, III           B. V, II, IV, III, I
        C. I, IV, III, II, V           D. III, V, II, IV, I

12.      I. They do not consider the problems correctable within   12.___
            the existing subsidy formula and social policy of
            accepting all eligible applicants regardless of
            social behavior and lifestyle.
        II. A recent survey, however, indicated that tenants
            believe these problems correctable by local housing
            authorities and management within the existing
            financial formula.
       III. Many of the problems and complaints concerning public
            housing management and design have created resentment
            between the tenant and the landlord.
        IV. This same survey indicated that administrators and
            managers do not agree with the tenants.

     The CORRECT answer is:
        A. II, I, III, IV              B. I, III, IV, II
        C. III, II, IV, I              D. IV, II, I, III

13.       I. In single-family residences, there is usually enough   13.___
distance between tenants to prevent occupants from
annoying one another.
  II. For example, a certain small percentage of tenant
families has one or more members addicted to alcohol.
 III. While managers believe in the right of individuals
to live as they choose, the manager becomes concerned
when the pattern of living jeopardizes others' rights.
  IV. Still others turn night into day, staging lusty enter-
tainments which carry on into the hours when most
tenants are trying to sleep.
   V. In apartment buildings, however, tenants live so
closely together that any misbehavior can result in
unpleasant living conditions.
  VI. Other families engage in violent argument.

The CORRECT answer is:
  A. III, II, V, IV, VI, I     B. I, V, II, VI, IV, III
  C. II, V, IV, I, III, VI     D. IV, II, V, VI, III, I

14.       I. Congress made the commitment explicit in the Housing   14.___
Act of 1949, establishing as a national goal the
realization of *a decent home and suitable environment for every American family.*
  II. The result has been that the goal of decent home and
suitable environment is still as far distant as ever
for the disadvantaged urban family.
 III. In spite of this action by Congress, federal housing
programs have continued to be fragmented and grossly
underfunded.
  IV. The passage of the National Housing Act signalled a
new federal commitment to provide housing for the
nation's citizens.

The CORRECT answer is:
  A. I, IV, III, II     B. IV, I, III, II
  C. IV, I, II, III     D. II, IV, I, III

15.       I. The greater expense does not necessarily involve   15.___
*exploitation*, but it is often perceived as exploi-
tative and unfair by those who are aware of the
price differences involved, but unaware of operating
costs.
  II. Ghetto residents believe they are *exploited* by local
merchants, and evidence substantiates some of these
beliefs.
 III. However, stores in low-income areas were more likely
to be small independents, which could not achieve the
economies available to supermarket chains and were,
therefore, more likely to charge higher prices, and
the customers were more likely to buy smaller-sized
packages which are more expensive per unit of
measure.
  IV. A study conducted in one city showed that distinctly
higher prices were charged for goods sold in ghetto
stores than in other areas.

The CORRECT answer is:
   A. IV, II, I, III
   C. II, IV, III, I
   B. IV, I, III, II
   D. II, III, IV, I

---

# KEY (CORRECT ANSWERS)

1. C
2. E
3. B
4. D
5. D

6. C
7. A
8. B
9. C
10. D

11. D
12. C
13. B
14. B
15. C

---

TEST NO. _____ PART _____ TITLE OF POSITION _____
(AS GIVEN IN EXAMINATION ANNOUNCEMENT · INCLUDE OPTION, IF ANY)

PLACE OF EXAMINATION _____ DATE _____ _____
(CITY OR TOWN)                                    (STATE)

RATING

## USE THE SPECIAL PENCIL.   MAKE GLOSSY BLACK MARKS.

| | A | B | C | D | E | | A | B | C | D | E | | A | B | C | D | E | | A | B | C | D | E | | A | B | C | D | E |
|---|---|---|---|---|---|---|---|---|---|---|---|---|---|---|---|---|---|---|---|---|---|---|---|---|---|---|---|---|---|
| 1 | | | | | | 26 | | | | | | 51 | | | | | | 76 | | | | | | 101 | | | | | |
| 2 | | | | | | 27 | | | | | | 52 | | | | | | 77 | | | | | | 102 | | | | | |
| 3 | | | | | | 28 | | | | | | 53 | | | | | | 78 | | | | | | 103 | | | | | |
| 4 | | | | | | 29 | | | | | | 54 | | | | | | 79 | | | | | | 104 | | | | | |
| 5 | | | | | | 30 | | | | | | 55 | | | | | | 80 | | | | | | 105 | | | | | |
| 6 | | | | | | 31 | | | | | | 56 | | | | | | 81 | | | | | | 106 | | | | | |
| 7 | | | | | | 32 | | | | | | 57 | | | | | | 82 | | | | | | 107 | | | | | |
| 8 | | | | | | 33 | | | | | | 58 | | | | | | 83 | | | | | | 108 | | | | | |
| 9 | | | | | | 34 | | | | | | 59 | | | | | | 84 | | | | | | 109 | | | | | |
| 10 | | | | | | 35 | | | | | | 60 | | | | | | 85 | | | | | | 110 | | | | | |

Make only ONE mark for each answer.   Additional and stray marks may be
counted as mistakes.   In making corrections, erase errors COMPLETELY.

| | A | B | C | D | E | | A | B | C | D | E | | A | B | C | D | E | | A | B | C | D | E | | A | B | C | D | E |
|---|---|---|---|---|---|---|---|---|---|---|---|---|---|---|---|---|---|---|---|---|---|---|---|---|---|---|---|---|---|
| 11 | | | | | | 36 | | | | | | 61 | | | | | | 86 | | | | | | 111 | | | | | |
| 12 | | | | | | 37 | | | | | | 62 | | | | | | 87 | | | | | | 112 | | | | | |
| 13 | | | | | | 38 | | | | | | 63 | | | | | | 88 | | | | | | 113 | | | | | |
| 14 | | | | | | 39 | | | | | | 64 | | | | | | 89 | | | | | | 114 | | | | | |
| 15 | | | | | | 40 | | | | | | 65 | | | | | | 90 | | | | | | 115 | | | | | |
| 16 | | | | | | 41 | | | | | | 66 | | | | | | 91 | | | | | | 116 | | | | | |
| 17 | | | | | | 42 | | | | | | 67 | | | | | | 92 | | | | | | 117 | | | | | |
| 18 | | | | | | 43 | | | | | | 68 | | | | | | 93 | | | | | | 118 | | | | | |
| 19 | | | | | | 44 | | | | | | 69 | | | | | | 94 | | | | | | 119 | | | | | |
| 20 | | | | | | 45 | | | | | | 70 | | | | | | 95 | | | | | | 120 | | | | | |
| 21 | | | | | | 46 | | | | | | 71 | | | | | | 96 | | | | | | 121 | | | | | |
| 22 | | | | | | 47 | | | | | | 72 | | | | | | 97 | | | | | | 122 | | | | | |
| 23 | | | | | | 48 | | | | | | 73 | | | | | | 98 | | | | | | 123 | | | | | |
| 24 | | | | | | 49 | | | | | | 74 | | | | | | 99 | | | | | | 124 | | | | | |
| 25 | | | | | | 50 | | | | | | 75 | | | | | | 100 | | | | | | 125 | | | | | |

TEST NO. _____ PART _____ TITLE OF POSITION _____

(AS GIVEN IN EXAMINATION ANNOUNCEMENT - INCLUDE OPTION. IF ANY)

PLACE OF EXAMINATION _____ DATE _____

(CITY OR TOWN)                    (STATE)

RATING

## USE THE SPECIAL PENCIL.   MAKE GLOSSY BLACK MARKS.

|  | A | B | C | D | E |  | A | B | C | D | E |  | A | B | C | D | E |  | A | B | C | D | E |  | A | B | C | D | E |
|---|---|---|---|---|---|---|---|---|---|---|---|---|---|---|---|---|---|---|---|---|---|---|---|---|---|---|---|---|
| 1 |  |  |  |  |  | 26 |  |  |  |  |  | 51 |  |  |  |  |  | 76 |  |  |  |  |  | 101 |  |  |  |  |  |
| 2 |  |  |  |  |  | 27 |  |  |  |  |  | 52 |  |  |  |  |  | 77 |  |  |  |  |  | 102 |  |  |  |  |  |
| 3 |  |  |  |  |  | 28 |  |  |  |  |  | 53 |  |  |  |  |  | 78 |  |  |  |  |  | 103 |  |  |  |  |  |
| 4 |  |  |  |  |  | 29 |  |  |  |  |  | 54 |  |  |  |  |  | 79 |  |  |  |  |  | 104 |  |  |  |  |  |
| 5 |  |  |  |  |  | 30 |  |  |  |  |  | 55 |  |  |  |  |  | 80 |  |  |  |  |  | 105 |  |  |  |  |  |
| 6 |  |  |  |  |  | 31 |  |  |  |  |  | 56 |  |  |  |  |  | 81 |  |  |  |  |  | 106 |  |  |  |  |  |
| 7 |  |  |  |  |  | 32 |  |  |  |  |  | 57 |  |  |  |  |  | 82 |  |  |  |  |  | 107 |  |  |  |  |  |
| 8 |  |  |  |  |  | 33 |  |  |  |  |  | 58 |  |  |  |  |  | 83 |  |  |  |  |  | 108 |  |  |  |  |  |
| 9 |  |  |  |  |  | 34 |  |  |  |  |  | 59 |  |  |  |  |  | 84 |  |  |  |  |  | 109 |  |  |  |  |  |
| 10 |  |  |  |  |  | 35 |  |  |  |  |  | 60 |  |  |  |  |  | 85 |  |  |  |  |  | 110 |  |  |  |  |  |

Make only ONE mark for each answer.   Additional and stray marks may be counted as mistakes.   In making corrections, erase errors COMPLETELY.

|  | A | B | C | D | E |  | A | B | C | D | E |  | A | B | C | D | E |  | A | B | C | D | E |  | A | B | C | D | E |
|---|---|---|---|---|---|---|---|---|---|---|---|---|---|---|---|---|---|---|---|---|---|---|---|---|---|---|---|---|
| 11 |  |  |  |  |  | 36 |  |  |  |  |  | 61 |  |  |  |  |  | 86 |  |  |  |  |  | 111 |  |  |  |  |  |
| 12 |  |  |  |  |  | 37 |  |  |  |  |  | 62 |  |  |  |  |  | 87 |  |  |  |  |  | 112 |  |  |  |  |  |
| 13 |  |  |  |  |  | 38 |  |  |  |  |  | 63 |  |  |  |  |  | 88 |  |  |  |  |  | 113 |  |  |  |  |  |
| 14 |  |  |  |  |  | 39 |  |  |  |  |  | 64 |  |  |  |  |  | 89 |  |  |  |  |  | 114 |  |  |  |  |  |
| 15 |  |  |  |  |  | 40 |  |  |  |  |  | 65 |  |  |  |  |  | 90 |  |  |  |  |  | 115 |  |  |  |  |  |
| 16 |  |  |  |  |  | 41 |  |  |  |  |  | 66 |  |  |  |  |  | 91 |  |  |  |  |  | 116 |  |  |  |  |  |
| 17 |  |  |  |  |  | 42 |  |  |  |  |  | 67 |  |  |  |  |  | 92 |  |  |  |  |  | 117 |  |  |  |  |  |
| 18 |  |  |  |  |  | 43 |  |  |  |  |  | 68 |  |  |  |  |  | 93 |  |  |  |  |  | 118 |  |  |  |  |  |
| 19 |  |  |  |  |  | 44 |  |  |  |  |  | 69 |  |  |  |  |  | 94 |  |  |  |  |  | 119 |  |  |  |  |  |
| 20 |  |  |  |  |  | 45 |  |  |  |  |  | 70 |  |  |  |  |  | 95 |  |  |  |  |  | 120 |  |  |  |  |  |
| 21 |  |  |  |  |  | 46 |  |  |  |  |  | 71 |  |  |  |  |  | 96 |  |  |  |  |  | 121 |  |  |  |  |  |
| 22 |  |  |  |  |  | 47 |  |  |  |  |  | 72 |  |  |  |  |  | 97 |  |  |  |  |  | 122 |  |  |  |  |  |
| 23 |  |  |  |  |  | 48 |  |  |  |  |  | 73 |  |  |  |  |  | 98 |  |  |  |  |  | 123 |  |  |  |  |  |
| 24 |  |  |  |  |  | 49 |  |  |  |  |  | 74 |  |  |  |  |  | 99 |  |  |  |  |  | 124 |  |  |  |  |  |
| 25 |  |  |  |  |  | 50 |  |  |  |  |  | 75 |  |  |  |  |  | 100 |  |  |  |  |  | 125 |  |  |  |  |  |